Editor
Eric Migliaccio

Cover Artist
Marilyn Goldberg

Editor in Chief
Ina Massler Levin, M.A.

Creative Director
Karen J. Goldfluss, M.S. Ed.

Imaging
Rosa C. See

Publisher

Mary D. Smith, M.S. Ed.

ESSENTIAL SKILLS

Reading & Writing

GRADE 5

Includes Standards & Benchmarks

Bonus Parent Materials!
2 CD-ROMs
ENGLISH & SPANISH

- Features English and Spanish CD-ROMs with parent-support materials
- Develops student mastery of key concepts and skills
- Includes focused instructional and practice activities
- Great for pull-out, afterschool, and summer school programs!

ENI TRUSTED PARTNERSHIPS FOR STUDENT ACHIEVEMENT

Teacher Created Resources

Developed and Written by
Evans Newton Incorporated

Teacher Created Resources, Inc.
6421 Industry Way
Westminster, CA 92683
www.teachercreated.com
ISBN-13: 978-1-4206-6225-2
© 2009 Teacher Created Resources, Inc.
Made in U.S.A.

Teacher Created Resources

Table of Contents

Introduction

The *Essential Skills* series was developed in response to an overwhelming number of teachers frustrated by the fact that their students didn't have all of the skills needed to be taught the on-grade-level standards. Due to this dilemma, the staff at Evans Newton Incorporated reviewed the standards from national organizations (NCTM, NCTE, IRA, etc.) and many states to determine the top prerequisite skills that a student going into a certain grade level should know to be successful in that grade. The skills represented here are a compilation of many different states' standards and do not represent any one state's requirements. Since the introduction of skills vary slightly in some states, you may find it useful to also review and select *Essential Skills* books for the grade higher and the grade lower than you are teaching in addition to your own grade level.

The *Essential Skills* lessons were designed using the theories of many leading educational theorists. It is easy to see the influence of Madeline Hunter's *Essential Elements of Effective Instruction* used in the "Recall," "Review," and "Wrap-Up" sections. They were also designed using Grant Wiggins's Backwards Design Model, making sure the outcome and the assessment pieces were written before designing the actual instruction to go with them. In the questions included in the lesson, you will see many different levels from Bloom's Taxonomy represented, a reflection of the work of Benjamin Bloom.

As indicated before, the skills were written to cover skills taught at a previous grade level—generally just the preceding grade. The *Essential Skills* series was designed in a cumulative fashion—i.e., the skills from one grade level build on the skills from the previous grade level. If a student is multiple years behind, then going down to previous levels of the *Essential Skills* may be helpful. Please note that the lessons are meant to be review lessons that will help students activate prior knowledge. If students have never been taught the skill before, then the lessons will probably not be enough for the students to become proficient in the skill without further support.

Teachers from many different states and many different grade levels have found the *Essential Skills* to be very helpful at various times of the school year.

* Some teachers use the lessons at the beginning of the year to review important skills.

* Some teachers use the lessons throughout the year to introduce topics as they come up in their scope and sequence.

* Some teachers use the *Essential Skills* books for the next grade level following their state test as a way to prepare their students for the following school year.

In all of these situations, teachers have found the *Essential Skills* series to be helpful in building students' knowledge and preparing them to master the content that the states require students to know.

In addition to the classroom uses described above, books in the *Essential Skills* series have also proven to be effective tools for special programs such as after-school tutoring programs, summer-school programs, and Special Education programs where teachers need to solidify students' skills and help them progress towards excelling at on-grade-level content.

We truly hope that you enjoy using the *Essential Skills* books with your students and find them to be highly useful, as has been the case with the many teachers who have used them before you.

Standards Correlation Chart

Listed below are the McREL standards for Language Arts. All standards and benchmarks are used with permission from McREL.

Copyright 2006 McREL. Mid-continent Research for Education and Learning.

Address: 2250 S. Parker Road, Suite 500, Aurora, CO 80014. Telephone: (303) 337-0990.

Website: *www.mcrel.org/standards-benchmarks*.

Standards and Benchmarks	Skill # (Pages)
Standard 1. Uses the general skills and strategies of the writing process	
• **Benchmark 1.** Prewriting: Uses prewriting strategies to plan written work	Skill 23 (135-137); Skill 27 (156-160); Skill 28 (161-165)
• **Benchmark 3.** Editing and Publishing: Uses strategies to edit and publish written work	Skill 21 (123-127); Skill 22 (128-134)
• **Benchmark 7.** Writes expository compositions	Skill 27 (156-160)
Standard 2. Uses the stylistic and rhetorical aspects of writing	
• **Benchmark 3.** Uses a variety of sentence structures in writing	Skill 25 (143-147)
Standard 3. Uses grammatical and mechanical conventions in written compositions	
• **Benchmark 2.** Uses pronouns in written compositions	Skill 26 (148-155)
• **Benchmark 3.** Uses nouns in written compositions	Skill 26 (148-155)
• **Benchmark 4.** Uses verbs in written compositions	Skill 19 (112-117) Skill 24 (138-142)
• **Benchmark 5.** Uses adjectives in written compositions	Skill 20 (118-122)
• **Benchmark 6.** Uses adverbs in written compositions	Skill 20 (118-122)
• **Benchmark 10.** Uses conventions of capitalization in written compositions	Skill 21 (123-127)
• **Benchmark 11.** Uses conventions of punctuation in written compositions	Skill 22 (128-134)
Standard 4. Gathers and uses information for research purposes	
• **Benchmark 1.** Uses a variety of strategies to plan research	Skill 17 (99-104)
• **Benchmark 6.** Uses multiple representations of information to find information for research topics	Skill 18 (105-111)
• **Benchmark 7.** Benchmark 7. Uses strategies to gather and record information for research topics	Skill 17 (99-104)

Standards Correlation Chart *(cont.)*

Standards and Benchmarks	Skill # (Pages)
Standard 5. Uses the general skills and strategies of the reading process	
• **Benchmark 2.** Establishes a purpose for reading	Skill 11 (62-66)
• **Benchmark 4.** Uses phonetic and structural analysis techniques, syntactic structure, and semantic context to decode unknown words	Skill 3 (17-22)
• **Benchmark 5.** Use a variety of context clues to decode unknown words	Skill 2 (11-16)
• **Benchmark 7.** Understands level-appropriate reading vocabulary	Skill 1 (6-10)
Standard 6. Uses reading skills and strategies to understand and interpret a variety of literary texts	
• **Benchmark 1.** Uses reading skills and strategies to understand a variety of literary passages and texts	Skill 10 (56-61); Skill 16 (93-98)
• **Benchmark 2.** Knows the defining characteristics of a variety of literary forms and genres	Skill 16 (93-98)
• **Benchmark 3.** Understands the basic concept of plot	Skill 6 (33-38); Skill 8 (45-50)
• **Benchmark 5.** Understands elements of character development in literary works	Skill 3 (17-22)
• **Benchmark 7.** Understands the ways in which language is used in literary texts	Skill 12 (67-72)
• **Benchmark 10.** Understands the author's purpose or point of view	Skill 14 (79-83)
Standard 7. Uses reading skills and strategies to understand and interpret a variety of informational texts	
• **Benchmark 1.** Uses reading skills and strategies to understand a variety of informational texts	Skill 16 (93-98)
• **Benchmark 2.** Knows the defining characteristics of a variety of informational texts	Skill 16 (93-98)
• **Benchmark 3.** Uses text organizers	Skill 18 (105-111)
• **Benchmark 4.** Uses the various parts of a book	Skill 18 (105-111)
• **Benchmark 5.** Summarizes and paraphrases information in texts	Skill 5 (28-32); Skill 7 (39-44); Skill 15 (84-92)
• **Benchmark 7.** Understands structural patterns or organization in informational texts	Skill 13 (73-78)

Synonyms, Antonyms, and Homonyms

Skill 1: The student will determine synonyms, antonyms, and homonyms.

Instructional Preparation

Duplicate the following (one per student, unless otherwise indicated):

- "The Sun's Headdress" passage
- "Finding the Similar and Opposite Ones" handout

Prepare a transparency of the following:

- "The Sun's Headdress" passage
- "Finding the Similar and Opposite Ones" handout

Recall

Before beginning the **Review** component, facilitate a discussion based on these questions:

- ✳ When we talk about synonyms, what do we mean? (*words that have the same or nearly the same meaning*)
- ✳ Why would we use a synonym in a sentence? (*to make the sentence more interesting; to determine the meaning of an unfamiliar word; etc.*)
- ✳ When we talk about antonyms, what do we mean? (*words that have opposite or nearly opposite meanings*)
- ✳ Why would we use an antonym in a sentence? (*to make the sentence more interesting; to determine the meaning of an unfamiliar word; etc.*)
- ✳ How are finding and knowing synonyms and antonyms useful in reading? (*they help a reader understand the passage better; they enable the reader to determine the meanings of unfamiliar words; etc.*)
- ✳ When we talk about homonyms, what do we mean? (*words that have the same pronunciation, can be spelled differently, and have different meanings*)
- ✳ What strategies could we use to make sure we are using the correct homonym in a sentence? (*by looking at the context in which the word is used; by using prior knowledge and experience to see if the word is correctly used; etc.*)

Review

1. Make a T-chart on the classroom board by writing "Synonyms" in the first column and "Antonyms" in the second column. Then write on the T-chart the following words:

   - *error* and *mistake* in the synonym column
   - *loose* and *tight* in the antonym column

   Explain to the students that they are going to put their prior knowledge of synonyms and antonyms to use. Ask volunteers for examples of pairs of words that are synonyms, and write their responses in the synonym column. Ask the students why they think the words they have chosen are synonyms. Ask them for more examples. Go through the same process for antonyms. Discuss how synonyms and antonyms can be used to find the meaning of unfamiliar words or to determine the greater meaning of a passage.

Synonyms, Antonyms, and Homonyms *(cont.)*

Review *(cont.)*

2. Write the following words on the board:

   - creek
   - groan
   - soar

   Then ask the following questions:

   * What is the meaning of the word *creek*? (*a small stream of water running over the land*)

   * What word do you know that sounds the same as this word but has a different meaning and spelling? (*creak*)

   * What is the meaning of the word *creak*? (*the squeaking sound a door makes*)

   Record the responses on the board next to the word *creek*. Lead the students to understand that this word pair—*creek* and *creak*—consists of homonyms, and homonyms are words that sound alike but have different meanings and can be spelled differently. Continue this procedure with the remaining words (*groan* and *soar*). Tell students that in addition to finding synonyms and antonyms, they will be dealing with incorrect homonyms in a passage.

3. Distribute copies of "The Sun's Headdress" passage and display the transparency. Read the passage while the students read it silently.

4. Focus students' attention on the underlined words in the passage. Tell them to read each word silently. After they have had time to examine the underlined words, explain that each of these words will be used in one of three ways: to find a synonym, to find an antonym, or to find the correct homonym. Have them reread the words silently and determine which would be good to find synonyms for, to find antonyms for, and to fix with the correct homonym.

5. Distribute copies of the "Finding the Similar and Opposite Ones" handout and display the transparency. Have students locate the first underlined word in the passage: *peek*. Ask a volunteer to read the sentence in which the word *peek* appears. Then ask these questions:

   * What is the meaning of the word *peek*? (*to take a quick look*)

   * Is this word used correctly in the sentence? Why or why not? (*no, because Sun did not come down from looking at something, he came down from the mountain*)

   * What would be a better word, or homonym, to use in this sentence? (*peak*)

   * What is the meaning of this word? (*the top of a mountain*)

   Discuss the responses and write appropriate ones next to the word *peek* on the transparency. In the "Meaning" box, the meaning of the word *peek* should be written, and in the box labeled "Homonym," the word *peak* should be written. Have the students do the same on their copy of the handout. Continue this procedure with the next underlined homonym, *reins*.

Review *(cont.)*

6. Direct the students' attention to the word *immense* in the passage and have them place their fingers on it. Ask a volunteer to read the sentence in which the word *immense* appears. Then ask the following questions:

   ✳ What is the meaning of the word *immense*? (*very large*)

   ✳ What is a word that means the opposite of *immense*? (*tiny*)

   ✳ What is the meaning of this word? (*very small*)

   Discuss the responses and record them next to the word *immense* on the transparency. Have the students do the same on their copies of the handout. Lead the students to understand that *immense* and *tiny* are antonyms, indicating they have opposite meanings.

7. Direct their attention to the word *blazing* in the passage and have them place their fingers on it. Ask a volunteer to read the sentence in which the word *blazing* appears. Then ask the following questions:

   ✳ What is the meaning of the word *blazing*? (*brightly shining*)

   ✳ What is a word that means the same as *blazing*? (*glowing*)

   ✳ What is the meaning of this word? (*giving off light because of great heat*)

   Discuss the responses and record them next to the word *blazing* on the transparency. Have them do the same on their copy of the handout. Lead the students to understand that *blazing* and *glowing* are synonyms, indicating they have the same or nearly the same meaning.

8. Have the students get into pairs. Tell each pair to work together to complete the handout by completing the sections where the underlined word is given to them and then using the remaining six words to complete the sections of synonyms, antonyms, and homonyms. Remind the students that each of them is responsible for completing his or her copy of the handout.

9. Ask volunteers to share their responses from the handout. Discuss each response for accuracy, knowing that there may be multiple responses for each section. Record appropriate responses on the transparency.

Wrap-Up

- To conclude this lesson, have the students use the reverse side of the "Finding the Similar and Opposite Ones" handout to respond to the following questions:

  ✳ What is the function of a synonym and an antonym?

  ✳ How do we recognize homonyms?

- Ask several volunteers to read their responses. Facilitate a discussion that uses the responses to emphasize the importance of using synonyms, antonyms, and homonyms to understand a passage or determine the meaning of an unfamiliar word.

Synonyms, Antonyms, and Homonyms *(cont.)*

The Sun's Headdress

a myth from a South American Indian tribe

Long ago, Sun and Moon lived together on Earth. One morning, Sun woke up before Moon and decided to go walking by the river. He came down from the <u>peek</u> of the mountain behind which he had risen. The hard <u>reins</u> had made the river run very fast. When Sun reached the river, he saw a pair of woodpeckers on an <u>immense</u> palm tree. The two woodpeckers were busily pecking at the tree's trunk, and as Sun watched them, he could not help but notice the <u>blazing</u> red plumes on the birds' heads.

"I wish I had a gorgeous headdress like yours," said Sun in a <u>respectful</u> way. <u>Weather</u> or not he would get a lovely headdress would be up to the woodpeckers.

"You may have one of ours," said the woodpeckers as they kindly offered their gift to Sun. They hurled a plume toward Sun, and he stretched out his hand to catch the <u>valuable</u> gift. He did not realize that it would scorch his fingers! Sun <u>cautiously</u> juggled the plume up and down in the air until it was cool enough to place on his head. Then Sun positioned the plume <u>firmly</u> on top of his head and proudly walked home. When Moon saw the plume, he became envious and immediately wanted one for himself. Sun directed Moon to the spot where the woodpeckers were working.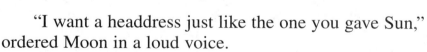

"I want a headdress just like the one you gave Sun," ordered Moon in a loud voice.

"We will give you one, but do not drop it," warned the woodpeckers. "This plume is the last one we have to give." Then the birds tossed the plume toward Moon. Sun hurried to help his friend catch the plume, but Moon told Sun <u>rudely</u>, "No! The plume is mine. I will get it."

Moon caught the hot plume but could <u>knot</u> hold on to it, and he dropped the flaming plume, which set the land on fire. The birds and the animals fled in fear to the edges of the Earth, and Sun and Moon climbed to the top of the sky where they are to this day—Sun with his <u>stunning</u> headdress and Moon with none.

Synonyms, Antonyms, and Homonyms *(cont.)*

Finding the Similar and Opposite Ones

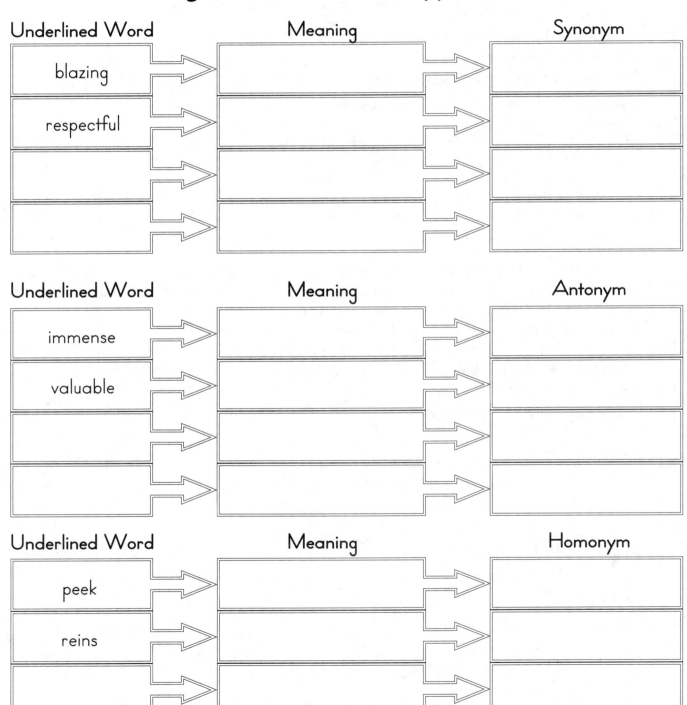

Underlined Word	Meaning	Synonym
blazing		
respectful		

Underlined Word	Meaning	Antonym
immense		
valuable		

Underlined Word	Meaning	Homonym
peek		
reins		

Words with Multiple Meanings

Skill 2: The student will interpret multiple-meaning words using prior knowledge, experiences, and context.

Instructional Preparation

Duplicate the following (one per student, unless otherwise indicated):

- "The Tennis Match" passage
- "What Do They Mean?" handout

Prepare a transparency of the following:

- "The Tennis Match" passage
- "What Do They Mean?" handout

Recall

Before beginning the **Review** component, start a discussion based on the following questions:

- ✳ What is a multiple-meaning word? (*a word that has more than one meaning*)
- ✳ What strategies can a reader use to determine the meanings of words with more than one meaning? (*look up the word in a dictionary or thesaurus; use context clues; use prior knowledge and experiences; etc.*)
- ✳ What are context clues? (*word clues, sentence clues, and paragraph clues that help tell the meaning of a specific word*)
- ✳ What is the advantage of using context clues to determine the meaning of a word with more than one meaning? (*it is more practical in a reading situation than looking it up; it does not take as much time as looking it up*)
- ✳ In what way do prior knowledge and experiences help determine the meaning of a word? (*They allow readers to use what they already know to determine the meaning of a word.*)

Tell the students that in this lesson they are going to be finding the meaning of multiple-meaning words in a sentence or passage using prior knowledge, experiences, and context clues.

Review

1. Write the following sentences on the classroom board:
   - Mary parked her car on the street close to the <u>curb</u>.
   - Peter needs to <u>curb</u> his spending so he can buy a new computer game.

   Read the sentences aloud as the students read them silently.

2. Ask the following questions:
   - ✳ What is the meaning of the underlined word in the first sentence? (*a concrete border that adjoins a street*)
   - ✳ What context clues helped you figure out this meaning? (*"parked her car on the street"*)
   - ✳ What prior knowledge or experiences led you to this conclusion? (*Accept all reasonable responses.*)
   - ✳ What is the meaning of the underlined word in the second sentence? (*to stop or control*)
   - ✳ What context clues helped you figure out this meaning? (*"so he can buy a new computer game"*)
   - ✳ What prior knowledge or experiences led you to this conclusion? (*Accept all reasonable responses.*)

Words with Multiple Meanings *(cont.)*

Review *(cont.)*

Explain that good readers figure out the meanings of multiple-meaning words by using context clues, prior knowledge, and experiences. Tell the students that if they are having trouble understanding a word in context, they can also look up the word in a dictionary or thesaurus. Tell them that in today's lesson they will practice using context clues, prior knowledge, and experiences to understand the different meanings of the same word.

3. Distribute copies of the "The Tennis Match" passage and display the transparency. Read the passage aloud while the students read it silently. Then ask a volunteer to reread the first sentence aloud while the rest of the students reread it silently. Ask the following questions and discuss the responses:

   * What is the meaning of the bolded word in the sentence? (*a small porch leading into a house*)
   * What context clues helped you figure out this meaning? ("*sitting,*" "*house,*" *etc.*)
   * What prior knowledge or experience helped you figure out this meaning?
   * What are other meanings that this word can have? (*to bend forward; to lower or degrade oneself*)

Distribute copies of the "What Do They Mean?" handout and display the transparency. Write appropriate responses in the correct spaces on the transparency. Have the students do the same on their copy. Explain that context clues help readers understand the meaning of a word if it is unfamiliar to them. Explain that the meaning of a word can come from the sentence or from the paragraph itself. Repeat this questioning sequence for the remaining sentences in the first paragraph of the passage.

4. Have the students get into pairs. Have them reread the passage silently. Explain that even though a word is spelled the same, it can have different meanings. Have the students work with their partner to complete the handout. Tell each pair to read each sentence carefully and then write the definition for each bolded word, the context clues and prior knowledge that led them to that definition, and other meanings of the word. Ask the students to think about where they might have heard the word before and what context clues they recognize that might help them know the word's meaning. The students may discuss their work, but each student should be responsible for completing his or her copy of the handout.

5. Ask volunteers to define the bolded multiple-meaning words in each of the sentences. As they define the words, write the responses on the transparency. Continue this procedure until all the words have been defined. Then have the students use what they have reviewed to figure out the meaning of each sentence. Discuss the responses.

Wrap-Up

* To conclude this lesson, have the students use the reverse side of their handout to respond to the following prompt: *What strategies can a reader use to determine the meanings of words with more than one meaning?*

* Ask several volunteers to read their responses aloud. Facilitate a discussion that uses the responses to emphasize the importance of interpreting multiple-meaning words using context clues, prior knowledge, and experiences.

Words with Multiple Meanings *(cont.)*

The Tennis Match

My friends and I were sitting on the front **stoop** of my house. We were trying to decide how to spend our Saturday afternoon. My buddies said we could go fishing or swimming or play baseball or tennis. I didn't want to play tennis because I didn't own a **racket**, but my friend Harvey told me that he had three or four and I could borrow one. I didn't complain or **object** because Harvey had extra tennis rackets and I thought playing tennis sounded like fun.

We walked to the tennis courts in our neighborhood. We had to wait only a few minutes before a court opened up. It was Harvey and I against Bob and Dylan. We had been playing for about 15 minutes, when some of the neighborhood kids came to watch us play. Since we weren't very good players, we tried to pretend we were. By pretending, we could **bluff** our way through the match. Harvey **stooped** to pick up the tennis ball. He threw the ball high into the air, and when it came down, he hit it as hard as he could with his racket. The ball lifted away and began its journey, but it never made it over the net! How can an **object** as small as a tennis ball get so **snarled** and tangled in the mesh of the net?

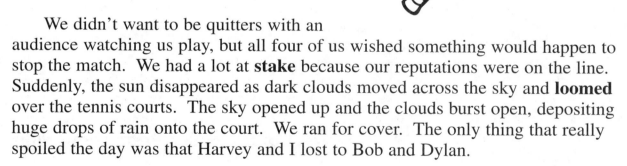

We didn't want to be quitters with an audience watching us play, but all four of us wished something would happen to stop the match. We had a lot at **stake** because our reputations were on the line. Suddenly, the sun disappeared as dark clouds moved across the sky and **loomed** over the tennis courts. The sky opened up and the clouds burst open, depositing huge drops of rain onto the court. We ran for cover. The only thing that really spoiled the day was that Harvey and I lost to Bob and Dylan.

Oh, well. There will always be another Saturday!

Name: _____

Words with Multiple Meanings *(cont.)*

What Do They Mean?

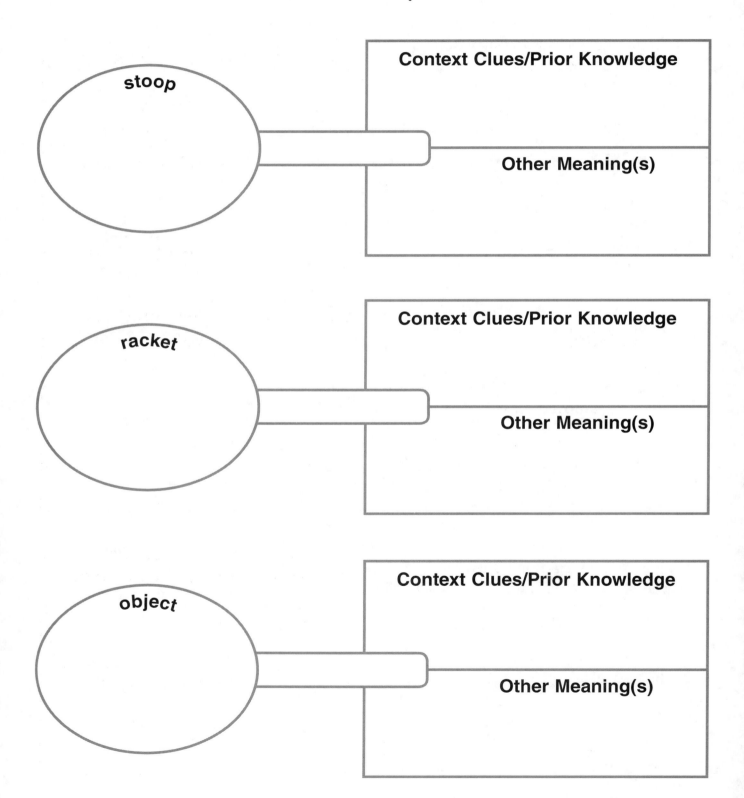

Words with Multiple Meanings (cont.)

What Do They Mean? (cont.)

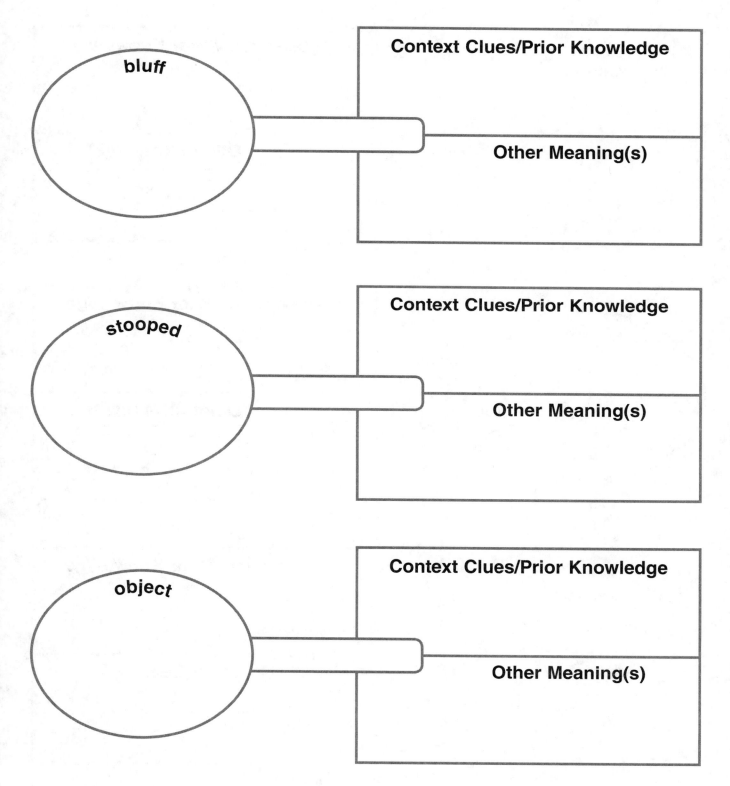

bluff

Context Clues/Prior Knowledge

Other Meaning(s)

stooped

Context Clues/Prior Knowledge

Other Meaning(s)

object

Context Clues/Prior Knowledge

Other Meaning(s)

Name: _____

Words with Multiple Meanings *(cont.)*

What Do They Mean? *(cont.)*

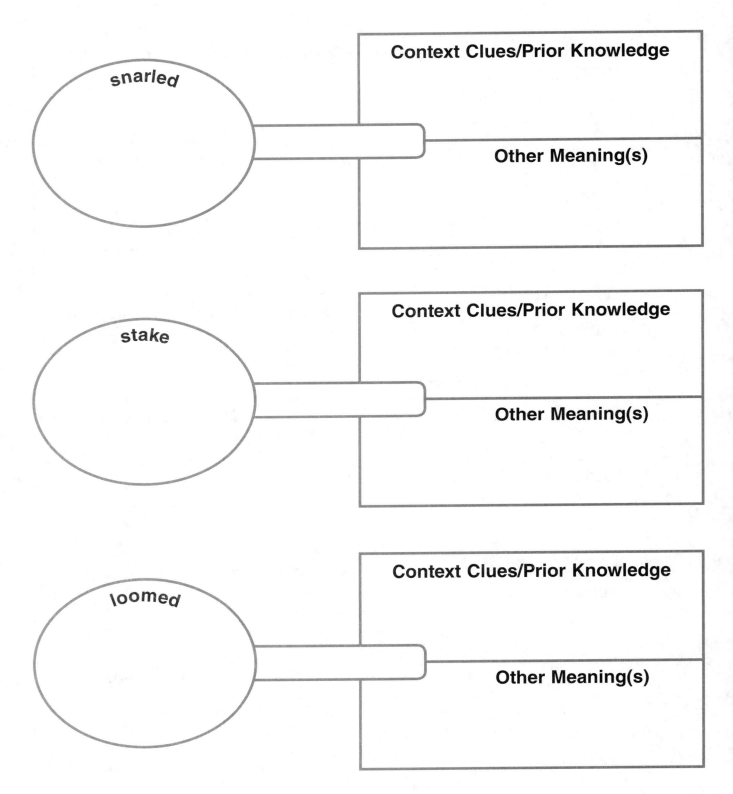

Identifying Root Words

Skill 3:   The student will use structural analysis to identify root words with prefixes (e.g., *dis-, non-, in-*) and suffixes (e.g., *-ness, -tion, -able*).

Instructional Preparation

Duplicate the following (one per student, unless otherwise indicated):
- "Root Words, Prefixes, and Suffixes" reference sheet
- "The Paper Girl" passage
- "Identify and Define" handout

Prepare a transparency of the following:
- "Root Words, Prefixes, and Suffixes" reference sheet
- "Identify and Define" handout

Recall

Before beginning the **Review** component, facilitate a discussion based on the following questions:

✳ What strategies can a reader use to determine the meanings of unfamiliar words? (*use a dictionary or thesaurus; use context clues; use knowledge of root words; use knowledge of prefixes and/or suffixes; etc.*)

✳ When we talk about root words, what do we mean? (*words that are the simplest form of a word and contain no prefixes or suffixes*)

✳ When we talk about prefixes, what do we mean? (*word parts that are added in front of a root word*)

✳ When we talk about suffixes, what do we mean? (*word parts that are added to the end of a root word*)

Explain to the students that they are going to be reviewing prefixes and suffixes and how they change the word's meaning when they are added to a root.

Review

1. Write the following words on the classroom board:
   - visible/invisible
   - agree/agreeable

   Read the words aloud as the students read them silently. Ask the following questions:

   ✳ What are the meanings of the words in the first set? (*the word "visible" means "possible to see"; the word "invisible" means "impossible to see"*)

   ✳ What caused the word to change its meaning? (*adding the prefix "in-" to the root or base word "visible"*)

   ✳ How did adding the prefix affect the meaning of the root word? (*the new meaning is the result of adding the prefix "in-," which means "not"; when the prefix "in-" is added to the root word, the meaning of the word changes*)

   Discuss the responses and write appropriate responses next to the word pair (*visible/invisible*).

Review *(cont.)*

2. Repeat this procedure for the words *agree/agreeable*. Lead the students to the understanding that when the suffix -*able* ("capable of") is added to the root word *agree* ("to be in harmony"), the new meaning is a combination of the root word and the suffix ("being able to be in harmony").

3. Distribute copies of the "Root Words, Prefixes, and Suffixes" reference sheet and display the transparency. Explain to the students that the reference sheet does not contain all of the prefixes and suffixes used in the English language. Tell them that the prefixes and suffixes that have been used on their reference sheet represent those that readers will see most often. Read the reference sheet aloud while the students read it silently. Discuss the prefixes and suffixes, their meanings, and the way in which each prefix and suffix combines with its root word to change the meaning. Ask volunteers to suggest one or two additional examples of words containing each prefix and suffix. Record their responses on the classroom board.

4. Distribute copies of "The Paper Girl" passage and the "Identify and Define" handout. Read aloud the passage while the students read it silently. Then ask a volunteer to reread the first paragraph of the passage aloud while the other students read along silently. Ask the following questions for the first bolded word (*attention*):

   ✳ What prefix or suffix do you see in the bolded word? (*the suffix "–tion"*)

   ✳ What does the prefix or suffix mean? (*"the result of"*)

   ✳ What do you think the word means? (*"the result of mental concentration"*)

   Discuss the responses. Then display the "Identify and Define" transparency and write the appropriate responses in the first row of ovals on the transparency. Have the students do the same on their copy of the handout. Follow this procedure with the remaining bolded words in the first paragraph of the passage.

5. Have the students get into pairs. Tell each pair to complete the handout using the bolded words in "The Paper Girl" passage. Tell them that they may refer to the "Root Words, Prefixes, and Suffixes" reference sheet for assistance. The members of each pair may work together, but each student is responsible for completing his or her own handout. Once the pairs have completed the handout, distribute dictionaries. Have the students look up the words in the dictionary to verify their meanings.

Wrap-Up

• To conclude this lesson, pose the following question: *Why is it important for a reader to understand prefixes and suffixes?*

• Ask several volunteers to share their responses. Facilitate a discussion based on the responses to emphasize the importance of recognizing prefixes and suffixes in words and the way the meaning changes.

Identifying Root Words *(cont.)*

Root Words, Prefixes, and Suffixes

What is a root word?

A *root word* is a word that is used as a base for making other words.

Examples: agree   bad   believe   even   fair   grace   help   hope

kind   like   love   pay   place   play   sick   view

What is a prefix?

A prefix is a word part that is placed at the beginning of a word, changing that word's meaning.

dis-	mis-	pre-	in-	non-
apart from; not; out of	wrong; bad; less	before	not	not; the opposite of

Examples: dislike = "not like"   misplay = "play badly"   inactive = "not active"

preview = "view before"   nonsense = "not making sense"

What is a suffix?

A suffix is a word part that is placed at the end of a word, changing that word's meaning.

-able	-ful	-less	-tion	-ness
able to; can do; likely to	full of; able to; likely to	without; not able to	the result of	state of being

Examples: believable = "able to be believed"   graceful = "full of grace"

hopeless = "without hope"   sickness = "being sick"

completion = "the result of being complete"

Identifying Root Words *(cont.)*

The Paper Girl

Mary thought about her decision. Was she going to breakfast with her friends or not? She thought she needed to pay **attention** to her paper route. Besides, she had a deadline to meet. Her mother always told her that she was **unstoppable** when it came to making money! It was unlikely that she would reconsider her decision, but Mary had to admit that sometimes she changed her mind. She thought for a little while, and then said, "I am not being **inconsiderate**; it is just **inconvenient**." Mary knew her friends would understand. She told herself that her friends' **happiness** didn't depend on her.

Mary's paper route began in the **darkness** before her friends even got out of bed. She had just started delivering her papers when a boy she thought she knew waved at her. He stopped and told her that her mother needed her at home. Mary asked him to watch her papers until she got back. She ran all the way back to her house, but her mother had already gone to work. Mary realized that he had tricked her. When she got back to her spot, Mary saw that her delivery wagon was empty. Her papers had **disappeared**.

Mary's father took her to the police station so she could give them a **description** of the thief. She was so angry; her **reaction** to the crook was shocking. "He was a sleazeball," she said. "I'd like to catch up with him. That boy was totally **dishonest**. Losing my papers is a real **disappointment**." Her mother patted Mary's hand. "It is **regrettable** that your papers were stolen, but you are a no-nonsense girl," her mother told her. "You will be back delivering papers before you know it!" Mary tried to explain to her mother that she was at a **disadvantage**. Her paper route would not be **profitable** until she could buy more papers to sell. She told the police that she was going to search for the mysterious stranger, but they told her that was **inadvisable**.

Mary and her parents started to leave the police station. At the same time they were going out the door, an officer was coming through the door into the police station. He was carrying her bundle of newspapers! "Where did you get those?" she asked.

"Some teenager handed them to me, telling me that he had **intended** to sell them, but they weren't really his to sell," the officer told Mary. Mary could have kissed the officer, but instead she thanked him, took her papers, and went back to her paper route.

Identifying Root Words (cont.)

Identify and Define

Prefix	Root Word	Suffix	Meaning

Identifying Root Words *(cont.)*

Identify and Define *(cont.)*

Prefix	Root Word	Suffix	Meaning

Analyzing Characters

Skill 4:   The student will analyze characters' traits, motivations, conflicts, points of view, and relationships.

Instructional Preparation

Duplicate the following (one per student, unless otherwise indicated):

- "The Tall Tower" passage

- "The Most Important Lesson" passage

- "A Character" handout (*one per three-student group*)

Prepare a transparency of the following:

- "A Character" handout

Recall

Before beginning the **Review** component, facilitate a discussion based on the following questions:

✯   When we talk about describing a character in a fictional passage, to what are we referring? (*describing the character's traits, motivation, conflicts, point of view, and relationships*)

✯   What are character traits? (*individual qualities a character possesses, such as his or her being honest and trusting, behaviors, looks, etc.*)

✯   What are character motivations? (*the reasons a character acts or reacts as he or she does in a story*)

✯   What are character conflicts? (*the problems a character encounters in a story*)

✯   What is a character's point of view? (*the way the character feels about or perceives actions and events in a story*)

✯   What are character relationships? (*the interactions among characters and the feelings that characters have about each other in a story*)

✯   Why is it important to be able to describe the characters in a story? (*to better understand the characters and why they act the way they do in a story*)

Review

1.   Distribute copies of the "The Tall Tower" passage. Read the passage aloud while the students read it silently. Ask the following questions (below and on page 24):

✯   Who is the main character in the story? (*King Carl*)

✯   What are the traits of this character? (*greedy, demanding*)

Analyzing Characters (cont.)

Review (cont.)

  ✳ What are this character's actions? (*King Carl wants to add the moon to the royal treasury; he demands that the royal advisors bring him the wisest person in the kingdom besides him; he commands his advisors to take a barrel off the bottom of the tower, even though they try to warn him of the danger.*)

  ✳ Why is the main character doing these actions? (*King Carl is determined to get all the gold and precious jewels.*)

  ✳ What conflicts does this character encounter? (*King Carl's advisors tell him he cannot reach the moon; King Carl is not able to reach the moon by climbing the tall tower.*)

  ✳ How does the main character feel about what is happening in the story or what is his point of view? (*King Carl becomes angry when he is told he cannot reach the moon; he becomes demanding when the barrels do not create a tall enough tower for him to reach the moon; he believes the moon belongs to him; he believes he can reach the moon if he has just one more barrel.*)

  ✳ What is the relationship of this character with other characters in the story? (*King Carl orders his royal advisors around and does not value their advice; he commands his advisors to do things they do not believe are right.*)

2. Display the "A Character" transparency. In a whole-group setting, ask the students to help you complete the transparency with an analysis of the character of King Carl. Ask them what you should put in the center box. Next, tell them to use the information discussed in the previous step to help you complete the rest of the ovals on the transparency. Write the descriptions in the appropriate ovals. Facilitate a discussion that leads to the conclusion that analyzing a character helps us better understand a passage.

3. Have the students get into groups of three. Distribute copies of "The Most Important Lesson" passage and the "A Character" handout. Have each group read "The Most Important Lesson" passage and then work together to complete the "A Character" handout using the same process you used together to analyze King Carl.

4. In a whole-group setting, ask volunteers to share what they wrote in the ovals and to explain how they arrived at their answers. You may want to ask students if they noticed how the character's traits, motivation, and point of view changed when he became an adult.

Wrap-Up

  • To conclude the lesson, have the students use the reverse side of their handout to respond to the following prompt: *What about a character do we need to analyze to help us better understand a story?*

  • Ask several volunteers to share their responses. Facilitate a discussion that uses the responses to emphasize the importance of analyzing a character's traits, motivations, conflicts, point of view, and relationships to better understand a story.

Analyzing Characters *(cont.)*

The Tall Tower

King Carl wanted the moon because he was sure it was filled with gold and precious jewels. He had a rule that all valuable things should belong to the smartest and greatest king in the universe. King Carl had passed that rule, since he considered himself to be the greatest. "I must add the moon to the royal treasury," he told his advisors.

"Impossible," said his first royal advisor. "Can't be done," said Advisor Number Two. Advisor Number Three told King Carl, "It's beyond your reach. If your royal hands can't touch it, neither can anyone else. The moon is very safe where it is—in the night sky!"

"Bring me the wisest person in the kingdom," King Carl said. "If I am to reach the moon, then I will need the best help I can get!" The royal advisors searched the kingdom far and wide. No one could help King Carl. The advisors were becoming very discouraged. They did not want to go back to the king empty-handed. As they sat on a rock near a field of sheep, a shepherd walked by and asked why they were so sad. The advisors explained their problem, and the shepherd said, "Is that all? My brother is the smartest man in the kingdom after the king because he knows everything there is to know about sheep. My brother can help King Carl."

The shepherd's brother and the royal advisors returned to the palace and went straight to the king. "Your highness," the first royal advisor said, "this shepherd will help you reach the moon."

"The moon?" asked the shepherd. "I thought you needed help with your sheep." The royal advisors looked at the shepherd and whispered to him, "If you do not come up with a plan, King Carl will throw us in the royal jail and no one will ever hear of us again." Suddenly, the shepherd had an idea to tell the king.

"Your highness, we have the answer!" said the advisors. "Have every subject bring all the barrels in the kingdom to the palace, and we'll have the royal carpenter tie them together into a tall tower. You can climb to the top and reach the moon." The king's subjects watched the tower grow and grow from the ground. Finally, King Carl said, "It is high enough! I will not wait any longer to climb to the moon." Then the king began to climb the tower. When he reached the very top of the tower, he stretched up to reach the moon. He could not reach it. "Send up another barrel so I can climb higher." The royal advisors told him there were no more barrels. The king was furious. He said, "Take a barrel off the bottom and throw it up to me."

"Your majesty, that is impossible. If we take a barrel off the bottom, the tower…"

"I command you to take a barrel off the bottom!" the king bellowed. So they pulled a barrel from the bottom of the tower!

Name: _____

Analyzing Characters *(cont.)*

A Character

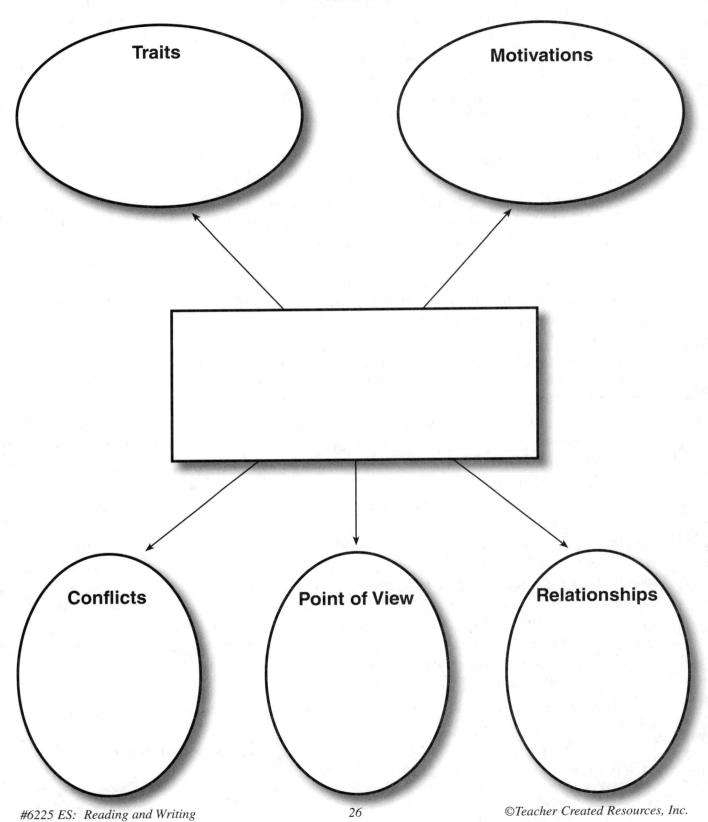

Traits

Motivations

Conflicts

Point of View

Relationships

The Most Important Lesson

When I was 13 years old, I thought I was a big shot. After all, I had reached the status of teenager, and I assumed that this made me mature enough to make my own decisions. I almost felt like an adult. Back then, what was important to me, however, should have been a clue that I wasn't quite an adult yet—in fact, I was far from it. I spent my time dwelling on clothes, hair, acne, sports, and friends. Had I been the adult I thought I was, I wouldn't have overlooked the most important aspect of my life at that time: my education. I learned a lot about myself through my friendships and all the stuff I dwelt on. However, I would have learned a lot more if I'd paid attention to my schoolwork. Back then, school wasn't a big deal to me. I felt that grades weren't important, either. I figured that if I wanted to go on to college, it was my high school grades that would matter. Now that I am older, I have realized that getting a grade is only one aspect of an education. There have been classes in which I received a good grade but learned little. There were classes in which I received a C and learned quite a bit. Education is really about learning. My fifth-grade history teacher, Mr. Ferris, taught this lesson to me.

Mr. Ferris was a rotund man with a black beard as thick as a steel-wool scouring pad. Most of the students disliked him; he was "too hard," they said. An "A" was not an easy accomplishment in Mr. Ferris's class. Aside from assignments out of the book, we were required to write long essays that analyzed important historical events, about which we knew or cared little. I now wish I had paid more attention. Mr. Ferris wasn't just pushing us so that we would meet his requirements for an "A" in his class. He was pushing us to dig deeper into the meaning of history and, as a result, the relevance of important events in history. In a nutshell, he wanted us to push ourselves to learn more. His motto was, "What doesn't kill you only makes you stronger." Well, at the time, what he was doing seemed to be killing me. I remember completing only about two-thirds of his assignments. They were just too hard, I thought. But now, as I look back on it, I wasted a wonderful opportunity. I didn't quite push myself hard enough at that critical time in my life. When I started high school four years later, I was already accustomed to taking the "easy route." I was unprepared for the rigors of classes like geometry and physics.

Nowadays, I look back on what Mr. Ferris tried to teach me. I always read and learn just for the pure joy of it. Learning is most definitely a reward in itself.

Comparing and Contrasting

Skill 5: The student will compare and contrast information in a passage(s).

Instructional Preparation

Materials:

- color photographs of both a panda bear and a koala
- highlighter (one per student)

Duplicate the following (one per student, unless otherwise indicated):

- "From China to Australia" passage
- "Bears Versus Bears" handout

Prepare a transparency of the following:

- "Bears Versus Bears" handout

Recall

Before beginning the **Review** component, facilitate a discussion based on the following questions:

- ✳ While reading, how do you compare information presented in a passage? (*by finding what is similar among the pieces of information about the two or more people, places, things, animals, objects, or ideas presented in the passage*)

- ✳ While reading, how do you contrast information presented in a passage? (*by determining the differences between the pieces of information about the two or more people, places, things, animals, objects, or ideas presented in the passage*)

- ✳ How do you find what is similar and different between two people, places, things, animals, objects, or ideas presented in a passage? (*by finding the related information about the persons, places, things, animals, objects, or ideas to determine if each piece is similar or different in any way*)

Review

1. Display the photograph of the panda so it is visible to all the students. Ask the following question:

   - ✳ What can you tell about pandas based on this picture? (*Responses will vary.*)

   Record the appropriate responses on a sheet of chart paper. Then take away the picture of the panda and display the photograph of the koala so that it is visible to all the students. Ask the following question:

   - ✳ What can you tell about koalas based on this picture? (*Responses will vary.*)

   Record the appropriate responses on another sheet of chart paper. Place the sheet of chart paper containing the information about the koala underneath its photograph. Then display the panda photograph and its corresponding information next to the other photograph and chart paper.

Comparing and Contrasting *(cont.)*

Review *(cont.)*

2. Ask the following questions:

* Which information is similar between the panda and the koala? (*Responses will vary.*)

* Which information is different between the panda and the koala? (*Responses will vary.*)

Discuss the responses and create and complete a Venn diagram using the appropriate responses to show how the panda and koala are similar and different based on the students' observations of the photographs. Tell the students that they will now read a passage about pandas and koalas to determine what is similar and different between the two animals.

3. Distribute highlighters and copies of the "From China to Australia" passage. Read the passage aloud while the students read it silently. Then ask volunteers to reread aloud assigned sections of the passage until they come across a similarity between pandas and koalas. On their copies of the passage, have the students highlight both sentences that contain the similarity. Then have the students skim through the section of the passage that has been read to find a difference between pandas and koalas. Ask a volunteer to share this difference, telling the students to underline the sentences containing the difference on their copy of the passage.

4. Distribute copies of the "Bears Versus Bears" handout and display the transparency. Show how to begin completing the handout by writing the difference underlined in the passage in the "Panda Bears" and "Koala Bears" sections and the similarity highlighted in the passage in the section labeled "What They Have in Common."

5. Have the students pair up. Tell each pair to reread the entire passage, underlining differences and highlighting similarities. Next, have them write the differences and similarities on the handout in the appropriate sections. The members of each pair may work together, but remind them that each student is responsible for completing his or her own handout.

6. Ask volunteers to share the similarities and differences they found between pandas and koalas. Discuss the responses for accuracy and have each volunteer write his or her response in the appropriate section on the transparency.

Wrap-Up

• To conclude the lesson, pose the following question: *How do you find what is similar and different among people, places, things, animals, objects, and ideas while reading a passage?*

• Ask volunteers to share their responses, facilitating a review about how to compare and contrast information in a passage.

Comparing and Contrasting *(cont.)*

From China to Australia

Giant Pandas

Giant pandas live in the mountain ranges of central China. They are found mostly in forests that contain bamboo. They are solitary animals, which means they mostly live alone. But pandas have been known to share their territory with a small group of other pandas.

The shape of a panda's body is similar to those of other bears, but pandas' bodies are covered in black and white fur. Black fur covers their ears, legs, and shoulders, and surrounds their eyes. The rest of their fur is white. Their fur is thick and wooly. It helps protect them from the weather.

Pandas grow to be 4 to 6 feet long. They can weigh up to 250 pounds. Their eyesight is very good, and they have sharp front teeth. These teeth help them bite off stalks of bamboo, which is mostly what they eat. Their large molars and strong jaws help crush the bamboo. Ninety percent of their food comes from bamboo, which makes them primarily an herbivore, or plant-eating animal. They eat sitting upright, holding the food with their front paws. Since bamboo is low in nutritional value, pandas eat 20 to 40 pounds of it per day. However, pandas do not need to drink much water. They get much of the water their bodies need from the bamboo they eat. Not only do they use their paws for eating, but they also use them for climbing trees. Pandas are good climbers. Their paws have five clawed fingers that help them grip the sides of a tree. They are sometimes seen napping high in the trees.

Panda cubs are born pink, hairless, and blind. They weigh about four ounces and are about the size of a stick of butter. They usually stay with their mother for about two years.

Pandas communicate with other pandas in many ways. They leave scent marks on trees and have 11 different calls for the occasional meetings with other pandas. Their call is like the bleating sound made by sheep or goats.

Pandas do not hibernate like other bears, and they do not roar. And while they may be cute and cuddly looking, they can be dangerous, even though they are a symbol of peace.

Comparing and Contrasting (cont.)

From China to Australia (cont.)

Koalas

Koalas are thought to look like living teddy bears. But this small, bear-like animal is not even a bear. It is a marsupial, like a kangaroo. Koalas live in Australia. They are found mostly in the tall eucalyptus-tree forests in the eastern part of the country. However, some are also found along the coastal regions and low woodland areas. Koalas are tree-dwelling animals, which means they live only in trees.

Koalas are ash gray in color, with tinges of brown in their fur. Their fur protects them from the weather. It keeps them cool in the summer and warm in the winter. Koalas grow to weigh about 20 pounds and are usually 24 to 33 inches in length. They have paws with five digits, each of which has a long, sharp claw. These claws enable them to climb trees with ease and grasp their food while eating.

The koala's diet consists entirely of leaves of eucalyptus (yoo ka LIP tis), or gum, trees. This means they are herbivores. Gum leaves are poisonous, so koalas are very picky about which kind of gum leaves they eat. Their highly developed sense of smell helps them detect which leaves are very poisonous and which are not. Their sharp front teeth help them nip the leaves from branches, while their molars help crush the gum leaves.

Koalas are nocturnal animals. This means that they are active only at night and during the dawn and dusk hours. They sleep about 18 hours per day to conserve energy. Some koalas may stay in the same tree for many days.

Koalas live in societies, like humans do. They share their "home range" territory with other koalas. To communicate, koalas use different types of calls. They make grunting noises when angry. They may scream and shake when scared. Mothers and babies communicate with soft clicking noises, squeaking sounds, and humming and murmuring. Koalas also mark trees with their scent.

Koalas may look like cuddly teddy bears, but these "bear-like" animals are more like kangaroos that don't hop or opossums that don't hang upside down by their tails.

Name: _____

Comparing and Contrasting *(cont.)*

Bears Versus Bears

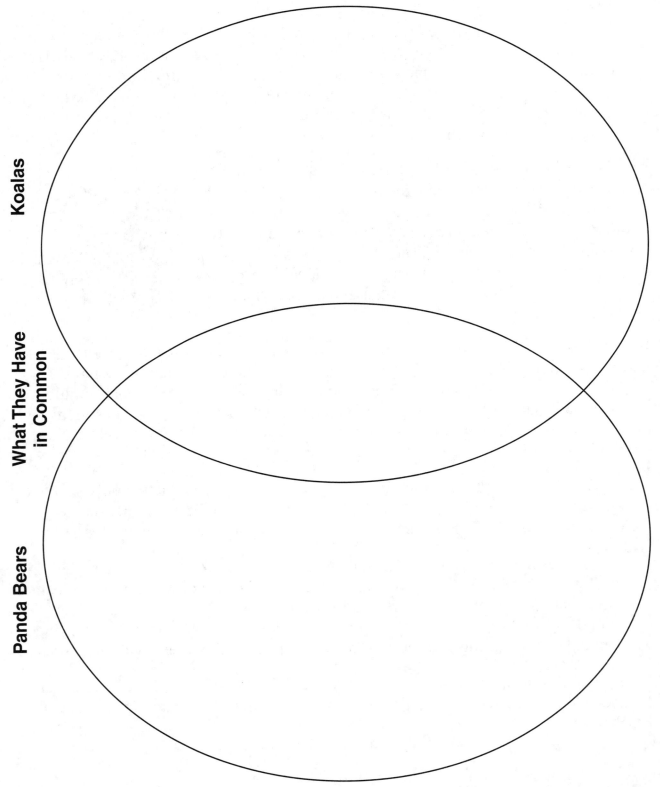

Koalas

What They Have in Common

Panda Bears

Sequencing Events

Skill 6: The student will correctly sequence the major events in a passage.

Instructional Preparation

Duplicate the following (one per student, unless otherwise indicated):

- "How the Fly Saved the River" passage
- "Story Sequencing" handout

Prepare a transparency of the following:

- "The Forgotten Ear of Corn" passage
- "Putting the Events in the Right Order" sheet
- "Story Sequencing" handout

Recall

Before beginning the **Review** component, facilitate a discussion based on the following questions:

- ✳ When we talk about sequencing the events in a story, what do we mean? (*We are referring to the order in which actions or events happen in the story.*)

- ✳ What questions should we ask to help order the events in a story? (*What happened first? What happened second? What happened next? What happened last?*)

- ✳ Why is it important to be able to sequence the events in a story? (*Being able to sequence the events in a story shows a reader's understanding of what happens in a story.*)

Review

1. Tell the students they will be putting the events of a morning in their correct sequence. Write the following in this order on the classroom board:

   - get dressed
   - eat breakfast
   - walk to school
   - wake up
   - go to class

   Ask the students to read all five items in the list and decide which activity they would logically do first and which they would do last, and then to think about how the rest of the activities best fit in order. Ask a volunteer to come to the board and write the number "1" next to the activity that is done first. Continue this procedure for the four remaining activities. Review the order with the students to make sure everyone is in agreement. Tell them that they will read a story and then place the events of the story in their correct order and sequence to show that they understand what happens in the story.

Sequencing Events *(cont.)*

Review *(cont.)*

2. Display "The Forgotten Ear of Corn" transparency. Read the passage aloud while the students read it silently. Discuss the important events in the story.

3. Display the "Putting the Events in the Right Order" transparency. Tell the students that they will now be putting the events in the story in the order in which they happened. Read the events in the right-hand column. Make sure all the events discussed in the previous step are on the transparency. Ask a volunteer to come to the overhead projector and draw a line from the word "First" in the left-hand column to the event that happened first in the story in the right-hand column. Ask the students how they decided that was the event that happened first. Confirm that the line goes to the corresponding event. Ask other volunteers to do the same for the remaining events listed on the transparency, each time asking the students to explain how they came to their decisions. Check the answers for accuracy. Remind the students that to correctly sequence the events in a passage, it is helpful to read through the entire list of events first. Then they should decide which event logically has to take place before all the others and what the logical progression is. Then they can review the passage and double-check their thoughts.

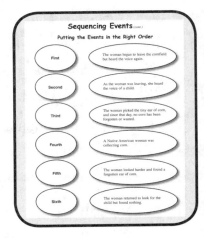

4. Distribute copies of the "How the Fly Saved the River" passage. Tell the students to read the passage silently. Then have the students get in pairs and reread the passage. Distribute copies of the "Story Sequencing" handout and tell each pair to work together to complete the handout according to the directions. The members of each pair may discuss the different events in the story, but each student is responsible for completing his or her copy of the handout.

5. Display the "Story Sequencing" transparency. Ask volunteers to share the events on their handout. Discuss the events for accuracy and record reasonable responses on the transparency.

Wrap-Up

- To conclude this lesson, have the students use the reverse side of their "Story Sequencing" handout to respond to the following question: *Why is it important for a reader to place events in a story in the correct order?*

- Ask several volunteers to read their responses aloud. Facilitate a discussion that uses the responses to emphasize the importance of being able to correctly sequence the events in a passage in order to better understand it.

Sequencing Events *(cont.)*

The Forgotten Ear of Corn

adapted from a Native American tale

A Native American woman was collecting corn one day. She wanted to have plenty of corn to last throughout the winter. She went from cornstalk to cornstalk and carefully tore off the ears of corn and placed them in her basket. When her basket was overflowing, the woman started to leave.

As she was walking away, she heard a tiny voice crying, "Please take me with you!" The woman was startled, for she couldn't believe that a child was lost in the cornfield. The woman put down her basket and returned to look for the child, but she could find nothing. So the woman started to leave again.

But again, she heard the tiny voice crying, "Please take me with you!" Again, the woman returned to the cornfield to search for the child.

Finally, in one corner of the field, the woman found a tiny ear of corn that was hidden by the leaves of the stalks. The woman knew at once that this tiny ear of corn had been crying out to her. The woman tore off the tiny ear of corn and placed it in her basket with the rest of the corn she had collected. Ever since, Native American women have carefully gathered their corn so that no ear is forgotten or wasted.

Sequencing Events *(cont.)*

Putting the Events in the Right Order

First

The woman began to leave the cornfield but heard the voice again.

Second

As the woman was leaving, she heard the voice of a child.

Third

The woman picked the tiny ear of corn, and since that day, no corn has been forgotten or wasted.

Fourth

A Native American woman was collecting corn.

Fifth

The woman looked harder and found a forgotten ear of corn.

Sixth

The woman returned to look for the child but found nothing.

How the Fly Saved the River

adapted from a Native American tale

A long time ago when the world was brand new, there was a magnificent river that sparkled in the sun. Many fish lived in the river, and all the animals drank from the river because its water was so dazzling and delicious.

A large moose found out about the river, and he went there to drink. But this moose was so gigantic that he drank so much that the water level began to sink lower and lower.

All the animals were worried. The beavers noticed that the water near their homes was vanishing. They knew that if this continued, their homes would be ruined. The fish were especially worried. They knew that the other animals could live on the land, but they could live only in the water.

The animals gathered for a meeting because they knew something needed to be done about the moose. For many hours the animals tried to think of a way to make the moose leave the river. They were unable to come up with a good plan—and even if they had, they were all too scared to approach the moose anyway. Even the bear, the largest animal at the meeting, was afraid of the moose.

Finally, the fly spoke up and said he would try to make the moose leave the river. All the other animals just laughed and called the fly crazy. They didn't think that the smallest of the animals could make a difference. But the fly did not respond to the animals, because he was confident in the plan he had come up with.

Later that same day, the moose returned to the river, and the fly knew it was time to put his plan into action. He flew over to the moose and landed on his leg and bit him. The moose reacted to this sharp pain by stamping his foot. As he stamped, the ground sank and water filled it in. The fly continued biting the moose on his leg, and each time the moose reacted in the same way. The river was quickly filling back up with water, but the moose still would not leave. So the fly jumped all over the moose and bit him each time he landed. This drove the moose crazy, and he ran all around the riverbank, stamping his feet harder and harder. Finally, the moose realized that he would never be able to get rid of the annoying fly. He ran away from the river and never returned again.

The fly was very happy that he had saved the beautiful river. He proudly said to the other animals, "Even the smallest of animals can make a difference."

Sequencing Events *(cont.)*

Story Sequencing

Directions: Write the nine most important events that happen in the "How the Fly Saved the River" passage in their appropriate boxes.

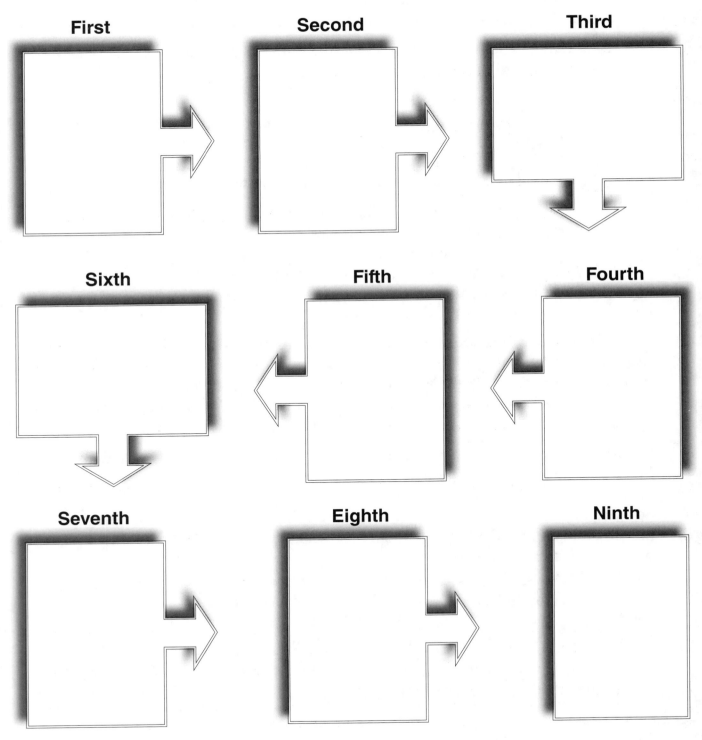

Main Idea

Skill 7: The student will describe the main idea and supporting details.

Instructional Preparation

Materials:

- highlighters (*one per student*)

Duplicate the following:

- "Captain Cook" passage (*one per student pair*)
- "What It's All About" handout (*one per student pair*)

Prepare a transparency of the following:

- "The Age of Exploration" passage
- "What It's All About" handout

Recall

Before beginning the **Review** component, facilitate a discussion based on the following questions:

✳ What is the main idea of a passage? (*what the passage is mainly about*)

✳ How do you figure out the main idea of a passage? (*by understanding the who, what, where, when, why, and how of a passage*)

✳ What are the supporting details in a passage? (*the information, facts, ideas, and/or sentences that support the passage's main idea; these details are the ones that are most important to understanding the passage*)

✳ How can you figure out the supporting details in a passage? (*by determining the most important information in the passage that helps defend the main idea*)

Review

1. Display "The Age of Exploration" transparency. Read aloud the passage while the students read it silently. Ask the following questions:

    ✳ What is the main idea of this passage? (*Exploration is actually one of the oldest human activities.*)

    ✳ How do you know this? (*The passage talks about exploration, and how and why humans did it.*)

   Discuss the responses, and circle the sentence on the transparency that contains the main idea. Explain that sometimes the main idea is stated in a passage, as in "The Age of Exploration," but other times the main idea may not be directly stated, it may be implied. When this occurs, it is up to the reader to use his or her understanding of the information in the passage to come up with a reasonable main-idea sentence that accurately describes what the passage is mainly about.

Review *(cont.)*

2. Have the students reread the passage silently, keeping in mind the passage's main idea. Ask the following questions:

   ❋ Which details in the passage support the main idea? (*"has been a driving force since the beginning of time"; "humans explored by land"; "also explored by sea"; "explorers had different reasons for traveling to the unknown"*)

   ❋ How do you know this? (*Responses will vary.*)

   Discuss the responses, underlining the appropriate supporting-detail sentences on the transparency.

3. On the classroom board, create a web to show the main idea and supporting details of "The Age of Exploration" passage. The center oval should contain the main idea, while the extensions from the center oval should contain supporting details. With the students' assistance, complete the web using the circled main-idea sentence on the transparency and the underlined supporting details. Discuss the web as it is being completed to make sure the students understand how to use a web to show the main idea and supporting details from a passage.

4. Have the students pair up. Distribute highlighters and copies of the "Captain Cook" passage and the "What It's All About" handout. Tell each pair to read the passage, determine the main idea, and highlight the supporting details. Then have them complete the handout by writing the main idea and the six most important supporting details.

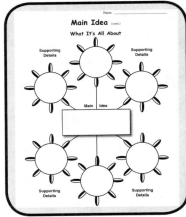

5. Display the "What It's All About" transparency. Ask volunteers to share their main-idea sentences and the supporting details. Discuss each for accuracy, writing appropriate responses on the transparency.

Wrap-Up

• To conclude the lesson, ask the following question: *How can a reader determine and describe the main idea and supporting details in a passage?*

• Give the pairs adequate time to discuss the question. Then ask volunteers to share their responses. Use the responses as a means to review how to find and describe main ideas and supporting details.

Main Idea *(cont.)*

The Age of Exploration

Exploration is traveling to unknown places to discover new things. It is actually one of the oldest human activities. Humankind's need to search the unknown has been a driving force since the beginning of time. In the past, people explored by land. They also explored by sea. But explorers had varying reasons for traveling to the unknown. Some did it for religious beliefs. Others wanted to set up new trade routes. Still others wished for fame, fortune, and adventure. The creation of better ships, weapons, and maps was important. It gave explorers the confidence to go out into the unknown world.

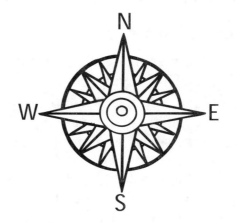

Main Idea *(cont.)*

Captain Cook

There were many explorers who sailed during the 18th century. But no one explorer was more successful than Captain James Cook. He discovered many islands in the South Pacific. He also achieved many things to help future explorers. He explored during three voyages to the Pacific Ocean and other voyages to places all over the world.

The Beginning

James Cook began his career as a seaman at age 26. He enlisted in the British Royal Navy. In the navy he learned to map areas of the world. He began by mapping parts of North America. But his real fame came from being a captain and an explorer.

Captain James Cook

Cook's First Voyage

Cook was made captain of the *Endeavour* in 1768. This voyage was planned for scientific reasons. Cook also wanted to search for *Terra Australis*. This place was the fabled southern continent. Many explorers believed it existed.

On August 25, Captain Cook and his crew set sail from England. They crossed the Atlantic Ocean. They continued around the southern tip of South America, Cape Horn. Their first destination was Tahiti. This island had good harbors. It also had friendly people and much food and water. After finishing the ship's scientific tasks, Captain Cook and his crew set course for the southwest. They sailed around New Zealand. Then they followed the eastern coastline of Australia. This was the first time a European had seen Australia. Captain Cook claimed this island for England. Then they headed back to England by way of the Cape of Good Hope. After passing the tip of Africa, Cook sailed for many months. Finally, his ship arrived back in England on July 13, 1771.

Captain Cook (cont.)

Cook's Second Voyage

On July 13, 1772, Captain Cook set out with two ships. These ships were the *Resolution* and the *Adventure*. Cook and his crew sailed around the Cape of Good Hope. Then they went south into the Antarctic Ocean. In January 1773, they crossed the Antarctic Circle. They could not continue to Antarctica because ice blocked the route. So, Cook decided to sail north to warmer waters. They sailed to Tahiti. After leaving this island, Cook discovered and explored many islands in the South Pacific. Easter Island, Vanuatu (van oo AW too), and the Marquesas (mar KAY sahs) were a few of these islands. After over three years at sea, Captain Cook and his crew returned to England. They reached home on July 29, 1775.

Cook's Last Voyage

During this voyage, Cook wanted to find the Northwest Passage. This passage was thought to be a way across North America. Cook and his crew set out in the *Resolution*. Its sister ship, the *Discovery*, came with them. During this expedition, Cook discovered the Hawaiian Islands. The natives of Hawaii thought Captain Cook was a god. After staying awhile, Cook and his crew sailed north up to Alaska and through the Bering Strait. Cook concluded that there was no Northwest Passage. They turned around and went back to Hawaii. When they arrived there, things had changed. Cook discovered that they had worn out their welcome. This led to the natives stealing one of the ships. In retaliation, Cook took a Hawaiian chief hostage. This caused the natives to become angry. They surrounded Cook and his crew. Cook was killed. Cook died on February 14, 1779. The ship returned to England without Cook. The crew arrived home on October 4, 1780.

Captain Cook was the first to map Australia. He charted much of the Pacific. He also discovered many islands. And he made it known that there was no Northwest Passage. All these actions led Cook to be known as a great explorer.

AUSTRALIA

Main Idea *(cont.)*

What It's All About

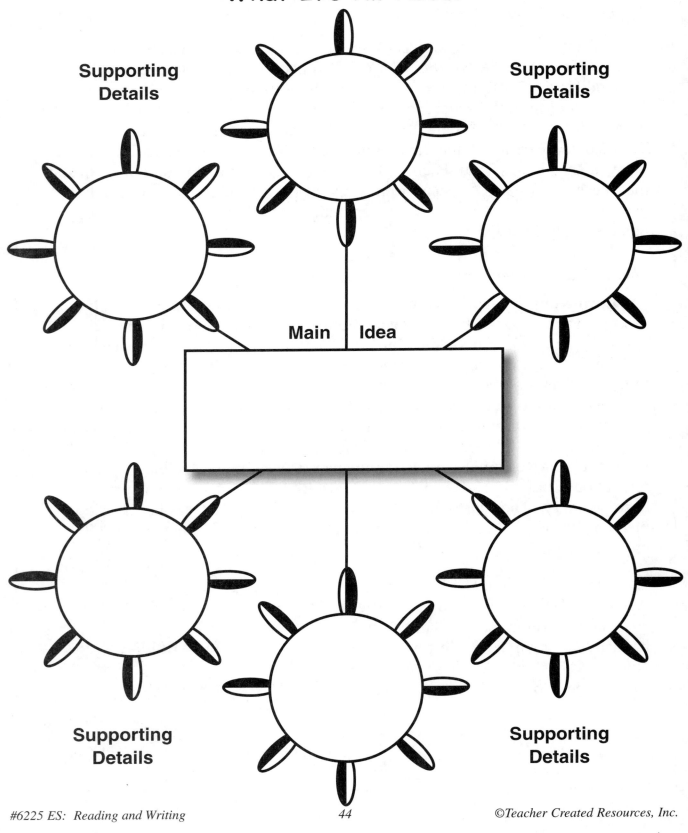

Supporting
Details

Supporting
Details

Main   Idea

Supporting
Details

Supporting
Details

Literary Elements

Skill 8: The student will describe the main literary elements of a fictional passage, including characterization, plot, setting, problem/resolution, and theme.

Instructional Preparation

Materials:

- overhead transparency markers, including the following colors: blue, green, red, purple, and orange (*for teacher's use*)
- sets of crayons or colored pencils, including the following colors: blue, green, red, purple, and orange (*one set per student*)

Duplicate the following (one per student, unless otherwise indicated):

- "A Slightly Damaged Promise" passage
- "Story Map: Describing the Elements" handout

Prepare a transparency of the following:

- "A Slightly Damaged Promise" passage
- "Story Map: Describing the Elements" handout

Recall

Before beginning the **Review** component, facilitate a discussion based on the following questions:

- ✳ What are the main elements that make up a fictional story? (*characters, a clear plot line, settings, problems and their resolutions, theme*)

- ✳ Who are the characters in a story? (*the people, or the animals or objects that often have human characteristics*)

- ✳ What is the plot of a story? (*the series of actions and/or events that build on each other throughout a story*)

- ✳ What is the setting of a story? (*the time and place in which a story takes place*)

- ✳ What are the problem and its resolution in a story? (*The problem is a conflict characters go through or encounter; the resolution is the point at which the main problem is solved.*)

- ✳ What is the theme of a story? (*the main message of a story; the moral of a story; the universal truth conveyed in a story*)

- ✳ What questions should you ask yourselves when trying to describe the characters, plot, setting, problem and its resolution, and theme of a story? (*Who is the main/supporting character? What is the character like? How does the character act? What is the sequence of events in the story? Which event was first? What did the character do at the end of the story? Where does the story take place? When does the story take place? What is the setting at the beginning of the story? What is the character's problem? How is the problem solved in the story? What is the theme of the story? What did you learn from reading this story?*)

Literary Elements *(cont.)*

Review

1. Have the students think back to the last fictional story the class read as a whole group. Ask the following questions:

    ✳ Who are the main characters in the story? Describe them.

    ✳ What are the characters like?

    ✳ How do the characters act?

    ✳ What is the sequence of events in the story?

    ✳ Where does the story take place?

    ✳ When does the story take place?

    ✳ What is the main character's problem in the story?

    ✳ How is the problem solved in the story?

    ✳ What did you learn from reading this story?

    You may vary the questions based on the story being used. Responses will vary; accept all reasonable responses. Discuss the responses for accuracy. Using the appropriate responses, create and complete on the classroom board or a sheet of chart paper a story map that has the following headings in this order: characters, setting, problem, plot, resolution, theme. For a sample of one type of story map, see the "Story Map: Describing the Elements" handout on page 50.

2. Distribute copies of the "A Slightly Damaged Promise" passage and the sets of crayons or colored pencils. Read the passage aloud while the students read it silently. Ask the following questions:

    ✳ Who are the characters in the story? (*Clarissa, Clarissa's mom, and Holly*)

    ✳ What are the characters' roles in this story? (*Clarissa is a girl who is angry at her best friend, Holly; Clarissa's mom is trying to cheer up Clarissa because Holly did not come over; Holly is a girl who has forgotten her promise to Clarissa about coming over.*)

    ✳ How do the characters act? (*Clarissa is angry and acts foolishly by blaming Holly for not keeping her promise; Clarissa's mom is sensitive to Clarissa's feelings and tries to convince her that Holly probably forgot about something she had to do that day; Holly is sorry for not coming over to Clarissa's house after school.*)

    Discuss the responses. Display the "A Slightly Damaged Promise" transparency, and then, using the responses, show the students how to identify traits of each character by using a blue transparency marker to underline key words and phrases in the story that help describe the characters. Have the students do the same on their copy of the passage using their blue crayon or colored pencil.

Literary Elements *(cont.)*

Review *(cont.)*

3. Continue asking questions about the setting, the plot, and the problem and its resolution, and the theme. Use the questions in the last star of **Recall** and **Step 1** of **Review** as possible questions. Underline information that helps describe the remaining elements in the following manner: underline the setting in green, the problem in red, the resolution in purple, and the theme in orange. For information regarding the plot, write numbers on the transparency showing the sequence of events in the story. Have the students do the same on their copy of the passage.

4. Distribute copies of the "Story Map: Describing the Elements" handout and display the transparency. Explain how to complete the handout by telling the students to describe the characters, setting, problem, plot, resolution, and theme in the appropriate boxes based on the underlined and numbered information in the passage.

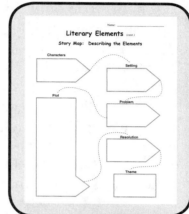

5. Ask volunteers to share their responses to each of the literary elements. Discuss the responses and record appropriate descriptions on the transparency.

Wrap-Up

- To conclude the lesson, have the students write on the reverse side of their "Story Map: Describing the Elements" handout a response to the following question: *What does a reader need to understand to be able to describe the main literary elements in a fictional story?*

- Ask volunteers to share their responses, discussing each one for accuracy. Use the responses to facilitate a review of how to describe the main literary elements in a fictional passage.

A Slightly Damaged Promise

Clarissa had just gotten home from school. She walked into the house excitedly, since it was Friday afternoon and her best friend and next-door neighbor Holly had said she would be coming over. Clarissa and Holly went to different schools: Clarissa went to a public school, while Holly went to a private school. The only time they really saw each other was the few hours between getting home from school and eating dinner (and on the weekends, of course).

On Thursday, Holly had promised Clarissa that she would come over right after school the next day. They had planned to play their favorite board game. But Clarissa had been home for over an hour, and there was no sign of Holly. Clarissa had gone over to Holly's several times, but no one answered.

Clarissa was sad and angry at the same time. She was sad because she had no one to play with, and she was also mad because Holly had lied to her.

Clarissa stared out her bedroom window toward Holly's house. "I'll be over right after school," she said in an angry, mocking voice. "Yeah, right, you'll be over. LIAR!"

Just as she yelled "LIAR!" Clarissa's mom walked into the room. "Who are you calling a liar?" her mom asked.

"No one," Clarissa said, embarrassed that her mom had heard her.

"Did the window lie to you?" her mom chuckled.

"No, Mom," Clarissa replied. "Holly said she would come over right after school, and she didn't come over!"

"Did you ever think she might have had a doctor's appointment or someplace she had to be?"

"Why didn't she tell me she had something else to do?" asked Clarissa. "She said she would be over, and she is not here!"

A Slightly Damaged Promise *(cont.)*

"Maybe she forgot," her mom replied. "You've made promises and then had to break them because something came up, haven't you?"

"Yeah," Clarissa agreed, "I guess you're right. Maybe she did forget about coming over."

"How would you like it if I played that board game with you?" her mom asked.

"Yeah!" cried Clarissa as she grabbed the game and ran out of her room toward the kitchen table, frantically setting up the game. "That would be great!"

About 10 minutes into the game, the phone rang. Clarissa's mom answered the phone, and then said to Clarissa, "It's for you." She put her hand over the phone and whispered, "It's Holly."

"Hello," Clarissa said with uneasiness in her voice.

"Clarissa, I'm so sorry about not coming over," Holly said before offering an explanation of why she wasn't at Clarissa's. "I had forgotten I had a dentist appointment after school when I promised to come over. Do you forgive me?"

"Of course I forgive you. I didn't think anything of it," Clarissa said as she winked at her mom. "Maybe you can come over tonight? My mom said since it is Friday night it would be OK if you came over and spent the night."

"Let me ask my dad; hold on," Holly said. A few moments later she came back on the phone and said, "My dad said it's OK."

"Great," Clarissa said excitedly.

"Then I'll see you tonight!" exclaimed Holly.

"Tonight it is!" agreed Clarissa. "Bye!"

"Bye!" chimed Holly, and they both hung up.

Name: _____

Literary Elements *(cont.)*

Story Map: Describing the Elements

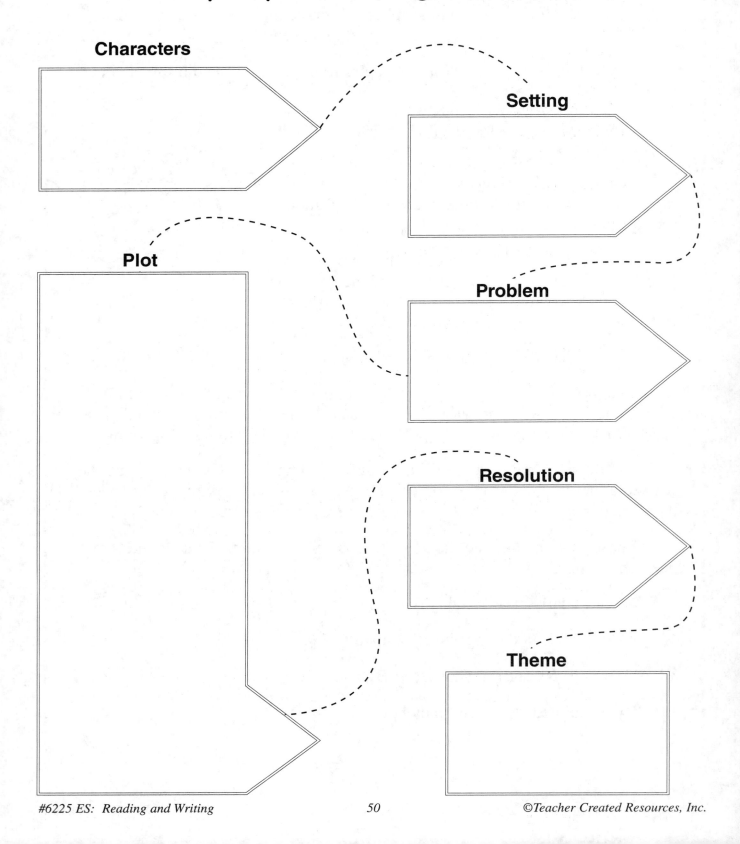

Characters

Setting

Plot

Problem

Resolution

Theme

Fact and Opinion

Skill 9: The student will distinguish between facts and opinions.

Instructional Preparation

Materials:

- light-colored crayons (one per student)

Duplicate the following (one per student, unless otherwise indicated):

- "Fact/Opinion Cards" sheet (one of each card per student)
- "Is That a Fact . . . or an Opinion?" handout

Prepare a transparency of the following:

- "Fact or Opinion?" sentence list

Recall

Before beginning the **Review** component, facilitate a discussion based on the following questions:

⁕ What is a fact? (*something that is actually true and can be proven*)

⁕ What is an opinion? (*what someone believes or feels is true*)

⁕ How do you decide whether a statement is a fact or an opinion? (*by making a decision on whether the statement is true or is just someone's thought or feelings about something; by looking for words like "best," "most," "believe," and "think" to determine that it is not a fact, but an opinion*)

Review

1. To begin the lesson, distribute fact and opinion cards. Tell the students they will be using the cards to show whether a statement is a fact or an opinion by holding a card up after a statement has been read. Write the following statements on the classroom board:

   - At over four miles in depth, Lake Baikal in Siberia is the deepest lake in the world.

   - The *Harry Potter* series by J. K. Rowling is the best set of books ever written.

2. Read the sentences aloud while the students read them silently. Ask the following questions (below and on page 52):

   ⁕ Is the first sentence a fact or an opinion? Raise the appropriate card showing what you think it is. (*fact*)

   ⁕ Why is this sentence a fact? (*The information in the sentence can be proven; you can look up the information in an encyclopedia, almanac, or atlas to see if it is true.*)

Review *(cont.)*

* Is the second sentence a fact or an opinion? Raise the card showing what you think it is. (*opinion*)

* Why is this sentence an opinion? (*It is what someone believes or thinks; someone may think that another set of books is the best, so this is someone's belief; it has the word "best" in the statement.*)

Discuss the responses for accuracy, leading to an understanding of why the first sentence is a fact and the second sentence is an opinion and how each is determined.

3. Display the "Fact or Opinion?" transparency. Tell the students that as a class they are going to read the sentences together and determine which are facts and which are opinions. Have them hold up their fact or opinion cards when they determine what the sentence is. Ask a volunteer to read the first sentence while the rest of the students read it silently. The students should hold up the "Opinion" card. Ask the following question:

   • What makes this a statement of opinion? (*It is someone's belief or thought; someone may not like the Spurs but may like the Lakers or the Celtics.*)

Discuss the responses, and color in the box labeled "Opinion." Continue this procedure with the remaining sentences on the "Fact or Opinion?" transparency.

4. Distribute crayons and copies of the "Is That a Fact . . . or an Opinion?" handout. Tell the students to complete the handout according to the directions. After they have completed the handout, ask volunteers to read each sentence, tell whether it is a fact or an opinion and explain why. Discuss the responses for accuracy.

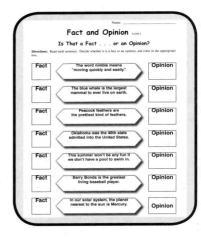

Wrap-Up

• To conclude the lesson, have the students use the reverse side of their "Is That a Fact . . . or an Opinion?" handout to write a response to the following prompt: *Write two facts and two opinions, telling why each is a fact or an opinion.*

• Ask volunteers to write their fact or opinion statements on the classroom board. Allow other volunteers to tell whether the statements are facts or opinions and explain why. Use the responses to review how to differentiate between facts and opinions.

Fact and Opinion *(cont.)*

Fact/Opinion Cards

Fact	Opinion
Fact	Opinion
Fact	Opinion
Fact	Opinion

Fact and Opinion (cont.)

Fact or Opinion?

Fact	**Opinion**	The San Antonio Spurs are the best basketball team in the NBA.
Fact	**Opinion**	Thomas Jefferson was the third president of the United States.
Fact	**Opinion**	That sunset was the most beautiful ever.
Fact	**Opinion**	Christopher Columbus is often considered the explorer who first discovered the Americas.
Fact	**Opinion**	The Declaration of Independence was signed on July 4, 1776.
Fact	**Opinion**	The best and most popular president ever to lead our country was Abraham Lincoln.
Fact	**Opinion**	The best way to understand what you have read is to retell the story to someone.

54

Fact and Opinion *(cont.)*

Is That a Fact . . . or an Opinion?

Directions: Read each sentence. Decide whether it is a fact or an opinion, and color in the appropriate box.

| **Fact** | The word *nimble* means "moving quickly and easily." | **Opinion** |

| **Fact** | The blue whale is the largest mammal to ever live on earth. | **Opinion** |

| **Fact** | Peacock feathers are the prettiest kind of feathers. | **Opinion** |

| **Fact** | Oklahoma was the 46th state admitted into the United States. | **Opinion** |

| **Fact** | This summer won't be any fun if we don't have a pool to swim in. | **Opinion** |

| **Fact** | Barry Bonds is the greatest living baseball player. | **Opinion** |

| **Fact** | In our solar system, the planet nearest to the sun is Mercury. | **Opinion** |

Stated and Implied Information

Skill 10: The student will draw conclusions based on stated and implied information.

Instructional Preparation

Duplicate the following (one per student, unless otherwise indicated):

- "What Good Is a Cat?" passage
- "Drawing Some Conclusions" handout

Prepare a transparency of the following:

- "What Good Is That Sack?" passage
- "Drawing Some Conclusions" handout

Recall

Before beginning the **Review** component, facilitate a discussion based on these questions:

* What is a conclusion? (*the ending; a reasonable opinion about someone, something, or a situation*)

* What does it mean to draw a conclusion when reading? (*to make a reasonable guess about someone, something, or a situation in a story based on evidence in the text and prior experiences and knowledge*)

* Why is it important to draw conclusions while reading? (*Conclusions help the reader better understand the deeper meanings in a story; conclusions enable a reader to better understand the characters and what is happening in a story.*)

* What types of conclusions are drawn while reading a fictional story? (*why a character does something; how the character feels; why the character chooses to react in a certain way; why the setting is important to the story; why an action or event is important to the story*)

* How can conclusions be proven reasonable? (*by finding words, phrases, and/or sentences in the story to support the conclusion; by using prior experiences and knowledge to logically support the conclusion*)

Tell the students that in this review lesson they will be learning how to draw conclusions about characters, places, and situations in a fictional story.

Review

1. Display the "What Good Is That Sack?" transparency. Read aloud the passage while the students read it silently. Ask the following questions:

   * What is this story mostly about? (*This is a story about Fox, who learns an important, yet late, lesson from Cat.*)

   * What conclusion can you draw about Cat's feelings about Fox? (*Cat admires Fox.*)

   * How do you know this? (*In the story it says Cat thought Fox was clever; in the story the word "chimed" is used to show Cat's tone when talking to Fox. This shows that Cat is happy to see Fox.*)

   * What conclusion can you draw about Fox's feelings about Cat? (*Fox does not care for Cat because he thinks that she is not smart.*)

Review *(cont.)*

❋ How do you know this? (*In the story it states that Fox does not like to talk to others who are not as smart as he is.*)

❋ What conclusion can you draw about why Fox stares at Cat before talking to her? (*Fox is deciding whether to talk to Cat.*)

❋ How do you know this? (*When others are staring at you in a conversation, it means they are thinking about something. In this case, Fox is thinking about talking to Cat.*)

❋ What conclusion can you draw about why Cat shares what she knows with Fox? (*Cat thinks what she has to say is important and that Fox will learn something from it.*)

❋ How do you know this? (*Cat is trying to be helpful because she may know that Dog is somewhere near.*)

❋ What conclusion can you draw about why Dog grabs Fox? (*Dog grabs Fox because Cat is too quick and jumps into the tree.*)

❋ How do you know this? (*The story states that "Cat quickly bounded into the high branches" while Fox just stood there.*)

❋ What conclusion can you draw about how Fox feels at the end of the story? (*Fox feels miserable.*)

❋ How do you know this? (*Accept reasonable responses.*)

❋ What conclusion can you draw about how Cat feels at the end of the story? (*Cat doesn't feel bad about Fox being caught.*)

❋ How do you know this? (*Accept reasonable responses.*)

Discuss the responses. Create and complete a web on the classroom board, similar to the "Drawing Some Conclusions" handout, in which the center oval is labeled "Conclusions" and the extensions from the center are the conclusions, with a second set of extensions providing evidence supporting the conclusions.

2. Distribute copies of the "What Good Is a Cat?" passage. Read aloud the passage while the students read it silently. Discuss the passage to determine what it is mainly about. Then have the students get in three-person groups. Tell each group to reread the passage together to figure out conclusions that can be drawn about it.

3. Distribute copies of the "Drawing Some Conclusions" handout. Have each student complete the handout based on the group discussion from the previous step. Each student should write four conclusions on his or her handout and support each with evidence from the passage or with prior experience and knowledge.

4. Display the "Drawing Some Conclusions" transparency. Ask volunteers to share their conclusions and evidence. Discuss each response for accuracy, writing four reasonable conclusions and their evidence on the transparency. If there are many reasonable conclusions, create and complete several conclusion webs on the classroom board to show these conclusions.

Wrap-Up

• To conclude the lesson, pose these questions: *What kinds of conclusions can be drawn from information in a story? Why is it important to draw conclusions while reading?*

• Ask volunteers to share their responses. Use the responses to review how to draw conclusions while and after reading a fictional story.

What Good Is That Sack?

adapted from the Grimm Brothers' fairy tale "The Fox and the Cat"

One day, Cat ran into Fox walking through the forest. She thought to herself how clever Fox was, so she decided to speak to him. "Good day, Fox!" chimed Cat. "How are you doing this wonderful afternoon?"

Fox had a very big head and did not like to talk to those he felt were lesser than he. He smugly stared at Cat from head to toe. Finally, after a few moments, he said, "Why should I stop and talk to you? I am much smarter than you. You have nothing of interest to tell me that I do not already know."

"You aren't as intelligent as you think you are," replied Cat. "I do have something to share with you that may help you someday."

"What do you have to share with me that I do not know?" asked Fox curiously.

"When Dog chases me," Cat stated, "I can jump into a tree to save myself from being caught."

"Is that all you have to tell me?" asked Fox, feeling very annoyed at what he had just heard. "I am the smartest of all creatures in this forest, and I have in my sack thousands of cunning ideas to keep me from harm."

Just as Fox was finishing his statement, Dog surprised Fox and Cat by appearing out of nowhere, directly in front of the two startled animals. Cat quickly bounded into the high branches of a nearby tree, while Fox stood, taken aback.

"Open your sack to save yourself," yelled Cat. But it was too late, since Dog had already seized Fox and was dragging him behind as he walked out of the forest. Cat yelled to Fox as he was gloomily being carted away: "Your sack of cunning tricks could not save you from Dog. If you could climb like me, you would not have been caught."

What Good Is a Cat?

adapted from the fairy tale "Puss in Boots"

Once upon a time, a man had three sons. The man passed away. He left the house and family business to his eldest son, a donkey to his second son, and a cat to his youngest son.

The youngest son, Duke, was upset over what his father had left him. He sat down near a stream and sighed, "What am I going to do with a cat!"

"Don't you worry, Master," the cat answered. "I will show you just how valuable I am. Give me a fine hat with a feather sticking from it and pair of magnificent boots, and I will show you what I can do." The cat dressed himself and went on his merry way, saying to his Master, "Do not look so miserable, Master. I will be back before you know I'm gone!" And the smartly dressed cat walked off into the forest to show his Master exactly how valuable he was.

In no time, the cat caught a beautifully plump rabbit and took it to a nearby castle. He knocked on the door, went before the King, and removing his hat and bowing to be polite, announced, "The Duke of Hazzard sends you this rabbit as a token of friendship."

The King thanked the cat for his gift and kindness, and the cat was on his way. The cat returned every day with a new gift for the King and his family. One day he brought partridges, and on other days he brought hares and skylarks. The Queen was very pleased with the gifts they had received and commented, "This Duke of Hazzard is a fine and courteous gentleman. He is very loyal to the King and his fiefdom, and we would like to meet him in the near future."

The cat arranged for the King, Queen, and the beautiful Princess to meet with his Master the day after next. But when Duke got wind of this, he was horrified that the King would discover that he was not rich, but a poor beggar. But the cat had a plan.

When the day came for the King and his family to meet Duke, the cat told his Master to jump into a nearby pond. When the King approached, the cat screamed, "Help, the Duke of Hazzard cannot swim. He is drowning!"

What Good Is a Cat? *(cont.)*

The King had his servants save the Duke from the pond and ordered that he be given new clothes.

"Wouldn't you like to marry a man as handsome as the Duke?" the Queen asked the Princess. "Oh, yes!" replied the Princess. "But does he live near this place?"

"He owns a magnificent castle and all the land that you see before you," the cat replied. "Come and see for yourself, and I will meet you there." With this, the cat hurried to a nearby castle, which was owned by a wicked and horrible Ogre. The cat knocked on the door, and when it opened, he bowed and removed his hat, saying, "My Lord Ogre, I come here to pay my respects to your greatness."

"What do you want from me, cat?" growled the Ogre.

"Sire, I have heard that you possess great powers," said the cat, "and have the ability to change into any great, large animal you wish."

The Ogre responded, "That is right; and so what?"

"Can you change into anything?" asked the cat.

"Anything!" roared the Ogre, growing impatient.

"Well, then," coaxed the cat, "can you turn into something as small as a mouse, because I do not think you can do it!"

"Oh, you don't, do you?" replied the Ogre. "Watch this," and he turned into a tiny little mouse.

In a flash, the cat pounced on the mouse and ate it up. Then he dashed to the castle gate just in time to let his Master and the King and his family in.

Needless to say, the King was very impressed with the Duke of Hazzard, and the Princess and Duke were soon married. They lived happily ever after. But from time to time, the cat would crawl up to his Master and whisper in his ear, "You see, Master, I am worth much more than a house, a family business, or a donkey!"

Stated and Implied Information *(cont.)*

Drawing Some Conclusions

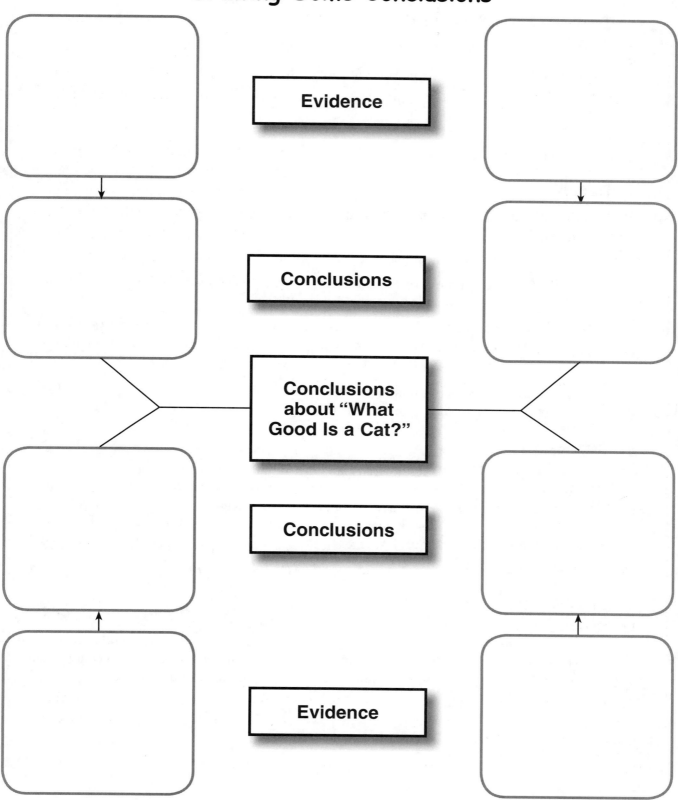

Evidence

Conclusions

Conclusions about "What Good Is a Cat?"

Conclusions

Evidence

Purposes for Reading

Skill 11: The student will establish purposes for reading (e.g., to be informed, to interpret, to be entertained).

Instructional Preparation

Duplicate the following (one per student, unless otherwise indicated):

- "Tell Me Why You'd Read This" handout

Prepare a transparency of the following:

- "Why We Read" page
- "Tell Me Why You'd Read This" handout

Recall

Before beginning the **Review** component, facilitate a discussion based on the following questions:

* Why do we read? (*Responses will vary; accept all reasonable responses.*)

* What are the main reasons that we read? (*to be entertained; to be informed; to interpret; to be persuaded*)

* Why is it important to know the reason that you are reading a passage? (*to know what you are looking for; to know what to focus on; to know which reading strategies to use to better understand what is being read*)

Tell the students that in this review lesson they will be reading to practice establishing the purpose for reading a particular passage.

Review

1. Display the "Why We Read" transparency. Read aloud the information on the transparency while the students read along silently. Discuss the purposes for reading to make sure the students understand each reason. Refer the students back to stories, passages, articles, textbook chapters, etc., that they have read recently. Ask the following questions for each text:

   * What is the reason we read [text title]? (*Responses will vary; accept all reasonable responses.*)

   * How do you know this? (*Responses will vary; accept all reasonable responses.*)

Discuss the responses to establish a reasonable purpose for each text and to determine how the students know this. Continue this questioning and discussion procedure with several different types of text that have recently been read in the classroom.

Purposes for Reading *(cont.)*

Review *(cont.)*

2. Distribute copies of the "Tell Me Why You'd Read This" handout and display the first page of the transparency. Direct the students to the "To Make a Prairie" poem, and read it aloud while the students read it silently. Briefly discuss the poem to determine what it is mainly about. Then ask the following questions:

   ✳ Why would you read this poem? *(to interpret; to be entertained)*

   ✳ Why do you think this? *(It is "to interpret" because you need to look deeper into what the author is saying; it is "to be entertained" because it is a beautiful poem and reminds me of being outdoors.)*

   Discuss the responses and model how to complete the graphic organizer next to the poem by writing on the transparency the appropriate response to the first question in the box labeled "The purpose for reading this is to . . ." and to the second question in the box labeled "I know this because . . ." Have the students do the same on their copy of the handout. Continue this procedure with the next passage on the transparency.

3. Have the students complete the second page of the "Tell Me Why You'd Read This" handout independently. When they are finished, display the second page of the "Tell Me Why You'd Read This" transparency. Ask volunteers to share their responses for each passage. Discuss the responses for accuracy, and write appropriate responses on the transparency.

Wrap-Up

• To conclude the lesson, ask the students to write a response on a sheet of notebook paper to the following prompt: *What are the reasons why people read? Explain each one and give an example of a passage you would read for that purpose.*

• Ask volunteers to share their responses. Use the responses as a means to review how to establish a purpose for reading.

Purposes for Reading *(cont.)*

Why We Read

To be entertained → We read to be entertained by fun, exciting, and humorous stories that let us use our imaginations.

We read to be informed so that we can find out information about the world and discover new things. ← **To be informed**

To interpret → We read to interpret so that we can better understand what we read and learn more about its meaning.

We read to be persuaded to buy things, to do certain things, and to understand others' points of view. ← **To be persuaded**

Purposes for Reading (cont.)

Tell Me Why You'd Read This

To Make a Prairie

by Emily Dickinson

To make a prairie it takes a clover

and one bee—

One clover, and a bee,

And revery.[1]

The revery alone will do

If bees are few.

_____

[1]daydream

The purpose
for reading this is to . . .

_____

_____

I know this because . . .

_____

_____

_____

Neptune

The purpose
for reading this is to . . .

_____

_____

I know this because . . .

_____

_____

_____

Eighth Planet from the Sun

Neptune is one of the planets in our solar system. It is over two million miles from Earth. It is the fourth-largest planet. It is the smallest of the four gas planets. These planets are Jupiter, Saturn, Uranus, and (of course) Neptune. These planets are made up mostly of hydrogen and helium gases. Neptune has a deep blue color. A vast ocean of water and rocky material covers the core, or center of the planet. A frozen layer of water and ammonia surrounds this. It is a windy planet. Ice crystals made of methane gas, which is poisonous, swirl around the planet. Neptune has four faint rings. It also has 13 moons.

Purposes for Reading (cont.)

Tell Me Why You'd Read This (cont.)

The purpose
for reading this is to . . .

_____

_____

I know this because . . .

_____

_____

_____

EAT AT

Angel's

Home of the
Triple Burger
Deluxe

HOT DOGS   Angel's   HAMBURGERS

Daily Specials!   Senior Discount

We have the best food in town!

Kids under 12 eat free every
Sunday, Tuesday, and Thursday

The Right Place at the Right Time

There once was a man named Cletus. Cletus loved to tell jokes. One day, while sitting in Angel's Diner, a man overheard Cletus telling jokes to some of the regulars. There was uproarious laughter coming from the corner of the diner. Everyone involved was having a wonderful time. They listened as Cletus poked fun at everything and everyone. The stranger walked over to the table and joined in the fun. He was impressed with Cletus and thought he was hilarious. The man turned out to be a TV executive. He offered Cletus a contract. Now Cletus is making the whole world laugh.

The purpose
for reading this is to . . .

_____

_____

I know this because . . .

_____

_____

_____

Figurative Language

Skill 12: The student will identify and describe figurative language such as metaphor, simile, imagery, and personification.

Instructional Preparation

Materials:

- highlighters (*one per student*)

Duplicate the following (one per student, unless otherwise indicated):

- "What Is Figurative Language?" reference sheet
- "Stars and Dreams" poem
- "Finding Figurative Language" handout

Prepare a transparency of the following:

- "What Is Figurative Language?" reference sheet
- "Name the Figurative Language" sheet
- "Stars and Dreams" poem
- "Finding Figurative Language" handout

Recall

Before beginning the **Review** component, facilitate a discussion based on the following questions:

✳ What are some different kinds of figurative language? (*metaphor (including simile), imagery, personification*)

✳ What is a metaphor? (*a direct comparison between two unlike things*)

✳ What is a simile? (*a type of metaphor that uses "like," "as," or "as if" to compare two unlike things*)

✳ What is imagery? (*language that appeals to the five senses*)

✳ What is personification? (*giving human qualities to things that are not human*)

✳ How can we identify figurative language in a passage? (*by looking for comparisons that are made; by finding things that are described with adjectives; by figuring out if the author is giving human qualities to any object; by finding words that appeal to the senses*)

✳ Why is it important to be able to identify figurative language in a passage? (*It makes the reader aware of the different ways authors describe things or the different ways things can be described.*)

Figurative Language (cont.)

Review

1. To begin this review, distribute copies of the "What Is Figurative Language?" reference sheet and display the transparency. Ask volunteers to read the definitions in the boxes aloud while the rest of the students read them silently. After each definition is read, have the students come up with their own examples of each kind of figurative language on a sheet of notebook paper. Ask volunteers to share their examples, then discuss them for accuracy.

2. Display the "Name the Figurative Language" sheet. Ask a volunteer to read the first sentence and identify what type of figure of speech it contains. Have the other students put their thumbs up if they agree with the volunteer's identification or down if they disagree. If there are any thumbs down, ask a volunteer to tell why he or she doesn't agree. Discuss each sentence until all students agree on the type of figurative language evident in the sentence. Then ask a volunteer to explain how they know it is the type of figurative language the class has decided on. Repeat this process with the remaining sentences.

3. Distribute the "Stars and Dreams" poem and display the transparency. Read the poem aloud while the students read along silently. Have students get in pairs, then distribute the highlighters. Tell the students to reread the poem and highlight any word or group of words that are examples of figurative language. Have each pair meet with another pair to compare highlighted parts of the poem. Have the students highlight any examples of figurative language in the poem they missed on the first go-around.

4. Distribute the "Finding Figurative Language" handout. Tell the students to complete the handout by writing examples of each kind of figurative language they find in the poem and by explaining how they knew that it was this kind of figurative language. Remind them to use their "What Is Figurative Language?" reference sheet as a guide.

5. Display the "Finding Figurative Language" transparency. Ask volunteers to share their pair's responses. Record appropriate responses on the transparency. Use the responses to facilitate a discussion that leads the students to a consensus on the different kinds of figurative language found in the poem.

Wrap-Up

- To conclude this lesson, have the students use a sheet of notebook paper to respond to the following prompt: *Write a description of a simile, a metaphor, imagery, and personification. Then write an example of each.*

- Ask several volunteers to read their responses aloud. Facilitate a discussion that uses the responses to emphasize the different types of figurative language discussed and how their use can enhance writing.

Figurative Language *(cont.)*

What Is Figurative Language?

Figurative language is language that contains figures of speech. In order to understand it, you must use your imagination. Some kinds of figurative language are metaphor, simile, imagery, and personification.

Metaphor makes a direct comparison between two unlike things.

Example: Justine was a rock during the fierce storm.

Simile is a type of metaphor that uses "like," "as," or "as if" to compare two unlike things.

Examples: Stacy's hair was like straw.

Her smile was as bright as a star.

He ran as if he were a rushing stream.

Imagery appeals to the five senses of sight, touch, sound, taste, and smell. Each sense helps paint a picture with words.

Examples: Her skin was leathery.

The snow looked like a white blanket covering the earth.

The screaming siren let me know the fire truck was on its way.

The sweet taste of chocolate filled my mouth when I bit into the cookie.

Walking into the bakery, I smelled the apples and cinnamon.

Personification gives human qualities to inanimate objects.

Example: The sun hugged me as I stepped outside into a warm summer day.

Figurative Language *(cont.)*

Name the Figurative Language

Directions: Look at the sentences below. What kind of figurative language is each an example of? Write the type of figurative language on the line provided.

Note: If the example is a metaphor that is also a simile, just write "Simile" on the line.

_____ 1. He was a lion in battle.

_____ 2. The wind whispered to the trees.

_____ 3. She is as pretty as a picture.

_____ 4. The blue sky was dotted with puffy, cotton-candy clouds.

_____ 5. The water balloon was as slippery as an eel.

_____ 6. He is a rock in his beliefs.

_____ 7. She ran like the wind.

_____ 8. The gift was as light as a feather.

_____ 9. The intense sun blared down on the dusty earth.

_____ 10. The seagull was a rocket as it dipped toward the water.

_____ 11. The tree waved in the wind like an old friend.

_____ 12. The moon is a spotlight, and the Earth is a stage.

_____ 13. Paper, pencils, and books were littered across his desk.

_____ 14. The flowers danced and played in the breeze.

Stars and Dreams

Trying to reach the stars

is as hard as climbing a mountain

when the wind bites your face

and the earth is covered

with a snowy white blanket.

But stars are dreams,

and dreams are

what life is made of.

So when the sparkling stars call to us,

shouting, "Reach me! Reach me!"

we must keep our dreams in mind,

plow our way through obstacles,

and grab those stars,

any way we can.

Name: _____

Figurative Language *(cont.)*

Finding Figurative Language

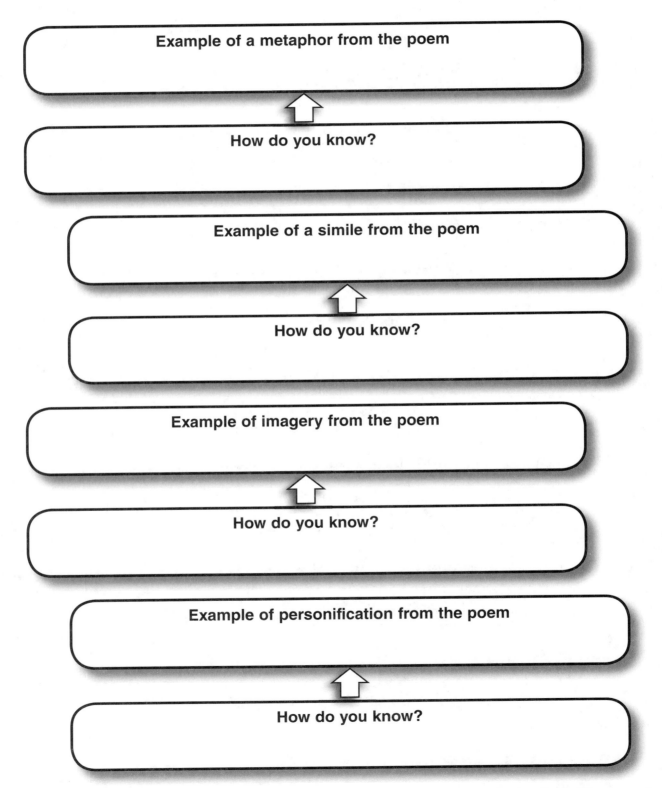

Example of a metaphor from the poem

How do you know?

Example of a simile from the poem

How do you know?

Example of imagery from the poem

How do you know?

Example of personification from the poem

How do you know?

Structure

Skill 13: The student will identify and describe the organizational structure of a nonfiction passage.

Instructional Preparation

Duplicate the following:

- "How It Is Organized" handout (*one per student pair*)

Prepare a transparency of the following:

- "Some Ways Authors Organize" reference sheet
- "Sample Passage"
- "How It Is Organized" handout

Recall

Before beginning the **Review** component, facilitate a discussion based on the following questions:

   ✳ What are the different ways in which authors organize a passage? (*cause and effect; chronological order; compare and contrast; problem and solution; order of importance; spatial order*)

   ✳ Why do authors organize passages in different ways? (*It helps a writer present information in a way that is appropriate to the topic about which he or she is writing.*)

Tell the students that in this review lesson they will be reading passages to practice identifying and describing their organizational structures.

Review

1. Display the "Some Ways Authors Organize" transparency. Ask volunteers to read aloud each of the four organizational structures while the rest of the students read along silently. Discuss each structure and ask volunteers to share examples they have read recently that characterize each of the structures listed on the transparency. Explain that *cause and effect* and *problem and solution* are closely related.

2. Display the "More Time" story from the "Sample Passage" page. Read the passage aloud while the students read it silently. Discuss the passage to determine what it is mainly about. Then ask the following questions:

   ✳ How does the author organize the information in this passage? (*problem and solution*)

   ✳ How do you know this is organized using a problem and solution structure? (*The author states the problem that the lunch period is too short and gives several ideas about how to solve this problem.*)

Review *(cont.)*

Discuss the responses and write the appropriate ones in the organizer below the passage on the transparency. Then ask the following questions:

* How would this passage be different if it were written using a compare-and-contrast structure?

* How would this passage be different if it were written using a chronological-order structure?

* How would this passage be different if it were written using a cause-and-effect structure?

Discuss the responses. (*Responses will vary; accept all reasonable responses related to the organizational structure addressed in the question.*)

3. Have the students get in pairs. Distribute copies of the "How It Is Organized" handout, and display the transparency. Read aloud "The Funnel Cloud" passage while the students read it silently. Ask the following questions:

* What is this passage mainly about? (*what tornados are, how they form, and what damage they do*)

* How does the author organize the information in this passage? (*cause and effect*)

* How do you know this is organized using a cause-and-effect structure? (*The author tells what causes tornados to form and what happens as the result of a tornado.*)

Discuss the responses. Write the appropriate responses in the organizer below "The Funnel Cloud" passage. Have each pair of students do the same on their copy of the handout. Then tell each pair to complete the handout by reading each passage and filling in the organizer below the passage.

4. Ask volunteers to share their responses. Discuss the responses for accuracy, and record the appropriate responses under each passage on the transparency.

Wrap-Up

* To conclude the lesson, have the students write a response on a sheet of notebook paper to the following prompt: *Describe four ways authors can organize a passage they write. Then write a sentence for each organizational structure that describes a type of passage that would be appropriate for that structure.*

* Ask volunteers to share their responses. Use the responses to facilitate a discussion regarding how to identify and describe organizational structures of passages.

Structure *(cont.)*

Some Ways Authors Organize

Cause and Effect

shows the cause of an
action or event and
then uses a number
of effects to help
explain the cause

Chronological Order

arranges details, facts,
and/or information
in the order in
which they occur

Compare and Contrast

shows the similarities
(what is alike) and the
differences between
two or more subjects

Problem and Solution

starts by a statement
of the problem and
then explores possible
solutions to the
problem or solves it

Structure (cont.)

Sample Passage

More Time

Our lunch period is much too short. The problem is not necessarily the entire time, since we get 45 minutes for our lunch period; it is the time we are given to eat. We are given 15 minutes to eat our lunch. Then we are sent out to the playground for recess. Fifteen minutes is not enough time. Sometimes it takes my friends and me 10 minutes to get through the lunch line. That only leaves us five minutes to eat. We are not given extra time because another class who has lunch after us needs to use the tables. One thing that would help would be to extend the time between classes coming in for lunch. If the class after ours came five minutes later, I probably would have plenty of time to eat. Another solution would be to set up tables outside on the playground. This would give those who are not finished with their lunches a place to go to finish eating. Whatever the solution is, I just want it to give me the opportunity to actually eat my entire lunch!

This passage is organized using _____

_____

I know this because _____

_____

_____

_____

_____

_____

Structure *(cont.)*

How It Is Organized

The Funnel Cloud

A tornado is a column of air that rotates violently. It extends from within a thundercloud. The funnel cloud must be in contact with both the ground and the thundercloud to be considered a tornado. Many tornados are formed in a special type of thundercloud. This is known as a supercell. A tornado starts when a current of moist, warm air rises up through the thunderstorm. The result of this activity is damaging. Tornados leave a path of destruction behind them. They have completely destroyed houses. They have flattened entire areas. They can lift up pavement and break it apart. They can also pick up cars and trailers and drop them someplace else. Even objects like sticks have been found driven into trees and brick walls.

This passage is organized using _____

I know this because _____

_____

_____

It's All in the Head

Some may think that alligators and crocodiles are the same. They are very different in many ways, but the differences are hard to see. One difference is the shape of their heads. Alligators have a wider, more rounded head. Crocs have a more pointed, narrow head. Since a croc's head is narrow, some of its teeth are visible when its mouth is closed. An alligator's teeth fit nicely in sockets in its mouth. Its teeth are visible only when its mouth is open. Another difference is that alligators prefer to stay in fresh water. Crocodiles have no problem venturing into either salt or fresh water. There are some kinds of crocs that live in salt water.

This passage is organized using _____

I know this because _____

_____

_____

Keep It Clean!

I don't know about you, but I hate trash and filth. Unfortunately, that is what we have been living next to for years. Rotary Park is in bad condition. The trashcans are overflowing. The grass is covered in garbage. The walls and buildings are covered with graffiti—most of which is not appropriate for our children. The playground is falling apart and is dangerous for our kids. Our community needs to pull together and restore the park to its original beauty. First, we need to write the city to demand that they clean it up. If that does not work, we need to take the lead. We will clean it up ourselves! We could organize several Saturday clean-up days. With the motivated people in this community, we will be able to reclaim our beautiful park.

This passage is organized using _____

I know this because _____

_____

_____

A Country Superstar

Garth Brooks was born February 7, 1962, in Tulsa, Oklahoma. Garth went to Oklahoma State University. He graduated in 1984. During his college years, Garth became a popular country music performer in the area. In 1987 he moved to Nashville, Tennessee. He wanted to be a country singer. The following year he signed a record contract with Capitol Records. His first album was released in April 1989. He began to get very popular after releasing his song "If Tomorrow Never Comes." It reached number one on the charts. He released his second album in late 1990. It sold over 16 million copies. Garth was now a country superstar. In 2000 he retired from country music, but not before selling over 100 million albums.

This passage is organized using _____

I know this because _____

_____

_____

ESSENTIAL READING & WRITING SKILLS

Author's Point of View

Skill 14: The student will identify the author's perspective or point of view in a nonfiction passage.

Instructional Preparation

Duplicate the following (one per student, unless otherwise indicated):

- "Bah Humbug!" passage

- "What a Mess You've Made" passage (*one per three-person group*)

- "His or Her Thoughts and Feelings" handout (*one per three-person group*)

Prepare a transparency of the following:

- "Bah Humbug!" passage

- "His or Her Thoughts and Feelings" handout (*two copies*)

Recall

Before beginning the **Review** component, facilitate a discussion based on the following questions:

✳ What is the author's perspective or point of view in a passage? (*the author's thoughts and feelings about the subject or topic of the passage; a message the author is trying to express to the reader*)

✳ How does an author express his or her perspective or point of view in a passage? (*by showing positive and/or negative points about the passage's subject or topic; by showing excitement or disappointment about the passage's subject or topic; by stating his or her opinions about the passage's subject or topic*)

✳ Why is it important to understand an author's perspective or point of view in a passage? (*It helps the reader recognize the intended meaning of a passage; it helps the reader understand the importance of the passage's subject or topic.*)

✳ What questions can a reader ask himself or herself to identify an author's perspective or point of view in a passage? (*Why did the author write this passage? What are the author's thoughts about the passage's subject or topic? How does the author feel about the passage's subject or topic? What is the author's opinion about the passage's subject or topic? How do I know this is the way the author feels about the passage's subject or topic?*)

Tell the students that in this review lesson they will read two nonfiction passages to practice identifying the author's perspective or point of view.

Review

1. Distribute copies of the "Bah Humbug!" passage, and display the transparency. Tell the students to think about the author's perspective or point of view while reading this passage. Read aloud the passage while the students read it silently. Discuss what this passage is mainly about.

Review *(cont.)*

2. Ask the following questions:

* Why did the author write this passage? *(to show his or her unhappiness with people trying to stop others from decorating their houses during the holidays)*

* Which sentences from the passage show the author's thoughts and feelings about decorating during the holidays? *("Most people enjoy seeing the lights that beautify the houses around the holiday season"; "It is our right as homeowners to adorn our houses the way we want to"; "As long as the lights are not too bright and the music, if there is any, is not too loud, then there should be no problem"; "It should be OK to decorate our houses any way we like"; "It is not right for those who don't like to decorate for the holidays to determine how others celebrate"; "Stop those who are trying to stop us from decorating"; "We are just trying to celebrate the holidays.")*

Discuss the responses. Underline on the transparency the appropriate sentences in the passage from the second question. Have the students do the same on their copies.

3. Display the "His or Her Thoughts and Feelings" transparency. On the transparency, write the sentences that describe the author's thoughts and feelings about decorating during the holidays in the box labeled "The Author's Thoughts and Feelings." Then ask the following questions:

* What is the author's perspective or point of view about people trying to stop others from decorating their houses during the holidays? *(The community needs to take action so the people in the neighborhood can keep decorating their houses the way they want to.)*

* How do you know the author has this attitude about decorating during the holidays? *(The author states how nice he or she thinks the decorations look; the author tells his or her opinion about holiday decorations; the author tells what he or she feels about the people who are trying to stop or limit the decorations.)*

Discuss the responses. Write appropriate responses for the first question in the box labeled "The Author's Perspective or Point of View" and appropriate responses for the second question in the boxes below the heading "How I Know This." Tell the students that this is the procedure they will be following to determine the author's perspective or point of view in another passage.

4. Have the students get in three-person groups. Distribute copies of the "What a Mess You've Made" passage and the "His or Her Thoughts and Feelings" handout. Tell each group to read the passage together and complete the handout.

5. After the handout has been completed, display another copy of the "His or Her Thoughts and Feelings" transparency. Ask volunteers to share their responses from the handout. Discuss these responses and record appropriate ones on the transparency.

Wrap-Up

* To conclude the lesson, pose the following question: *How can a reader determine the author's perspective or point of view in a passage?*

* Ask volunteers to share their thoughts. Use their thoughts to review what author's perspective or point of view is and what questions to ask to help determine the author's perspective or point of view in a passage.

Author's Point of View *(cont.)*

Bah Humbug!

a newspaper editorial from a local paper

The winter holidays are a wonderful time of the year. It is the time of the year when we all should be spreading holiday cheer. Whether we are Jewish, Muslim, Catholic, or Christian, each of us celebrates the holidays in his or her own way. Most people enjoy seeing the lights that beautify the houses around the holiday season. But there are some scrooges out there in our neighborhood. These people do not appreciate the lovely lights that light up the cold winter nights. There are people in our community who are trying to stop the decorations.

Lately there has been a push to limit the number of lights used during the holidays. This is wrong. There also have been people who want to limit the use of lights to inside the houses. This means no more lighted deer, Santas, or Christmas trees in the front yard. All this means no colorful light displays in your yard! This also is wrong. It is our right as homeowners to adorn our houses the way we want to. As long as the lights are not too bright and the music, if there is any, is not too loud, then there should be no problem. It should be okay to decorate our houses any way that we like.

It is not right for those who don't like to decorate for the holidays to determine how others celebrate. It is time for everyone in this community to step up. Stop those who are trying to stop us from decorating. We are not trying to cause problems. We are just trying to celebrate the holidays.

Name: _____

Author's Point of View *(cont.)*

His or Her Thoughts and Feelings

From the Passage

The Author's Thoughts and Feelings

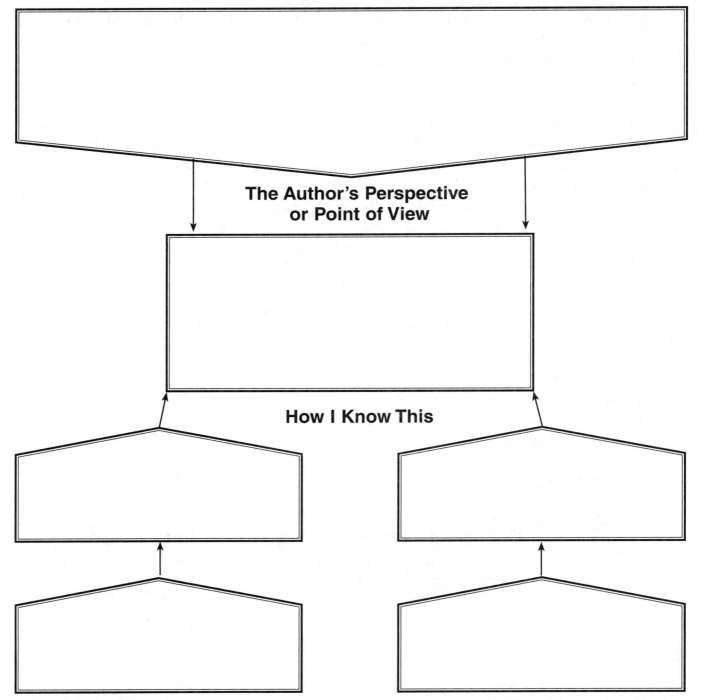

The Author's Perspective
or Point of View

How I Know This

Author's Point of View *(cont.)*

What a Mess You've Made!

a newspaper editorial from a local paper

Have you ever looked out your window and seen something you don't like? Well, I do that every day, rain or shine. What I see is something so hideous that it makes me sick to my stomach. Some of you in this area may know exactly what I am talking about. What I see out my window is Rotary Park—if you want to call it a park. It actually looks more like a garbage dump. There is trash everywhere. The trashcans are overflowing. I have not seen city workers come around to empty them in probably more than three months. The playground equipment is broken and unusable. The playground is actually a danger to the kids in the neighborhood. I've seen kids playing on the equipment, and I've seen kids get hurt playing there. The basketball courts also are unusable. None of the backboards have rims. One of the poles has actually fallen to the ground. Because of this, I do not allow my children to go anywhere near the park. But why do we have a neighborhood park if no one can use it? What should we do to make things better?

There are many things we, as a community, can do to solve this problem. The first thing we need to do is to write letters to the Parks Department. We need to state our concerns about the condition of the park. We can also attend the next city council meeting to state our concerns. The next meeting is a week from Thursday. But until our concerns are heard and acted upon, we need to take matters into our own hands.

If our concerns are not addressed, then we should set up a day to get together and clean up the park ourselves. The best place to start would be to empty the trashcans and pick up the trash that has spread across the park. We could also cut and care for the grass and take out the dead plants and replace them with new ones. I have already been in contact with Turner Nurseries, and they are willing to donate enough plants and gardening equipment to help make the park look beautiful. All we would need is people to volunteer to help their community.

A community clean-up day could then be scheduled. Please be part of the solution to this problem. It is time that we get together as a community and do something positive.

Paraphrasing and Summarizing

Skill 15: The student will paraphrase and summarize a passage to recall, inform, and organize ideas.

Instructional Preparation

Materials:

- 8½" x 11" blank, white paper (*one sheet per student pair*)

Duplicate the following (one per student, unless otherwise indicated):

- "Jump Right In!" passage
- "Writing What It's About" handout
- "Which Shall She Choose?" passage (*one per student pair*)

Prepare a transparency of the following:

- "Paraphrasing and Summarizing" reference sheet
- "Jump Right In!" passage
- "Writing What It's About" handout

Recall

Before beginning the **Review** component, facilitate a discussion based on the following questions:

❋ What does it mean to paraphrase a sentence or paragraph from a passage? (*to restate or reword a passage so the meaning is expressed in a different way*)

❋ Why is it important to be able to paraphrase a sentence or paragraph from a passage? (*to show comprehension of the information; to tell others specific information; to add details to a new passage to support an important idea*)

❋ What does it mean to summarize a passage? (*to rewrite the important information of a passage in your own words*)

❋ Why is it important to be able to summarize a passage? (*to better remember what was read; to tell others about the information contained in the passage; to arrange the ideas in a way that is easy to understand*)

❋ What does a reader need to know to decide which information to paraphrase and which information to include when summarizing a fictional story? (*what the story is mostly about; the characters in the story and their actions; the important events in the story; important information that should be summarized; important information that should be paraphrased*)

Tell the students that in this review lesson they will read fictional stories to practice paraphrasing and summarizing the information.

Paraphrasing and Summarizing *(cont.)*

Review

1. Display the "Paraphrasing and Summarizing" reference sheet. Ask volunteers to read aloud the "What is a paraphrase?" section of the reference sheet while the rest of the students read along silently. Discuss the information so that the students understand what it means to paraphrase.

2. Write the following sentence on the board:

   It was a dark, chilly night in the forest, as the wind was howling through the tall trees.

   Read the sentence aloud as the students read along silently. Ask the following questions:

   ✳ What is this sentence telling you? (*It was cold and dark in the forest.*)

   ✳ How would you best paraphrase this sentence? (*The wind blew the huge trees in the forest back and forth, making the air very cold on this dark night.*)

   Discuss the responses, and write an appropriate paraphrase of the sentence on the classroom board. Review how to paraphrase so that the students know how to paraphrase without plagiarizing.

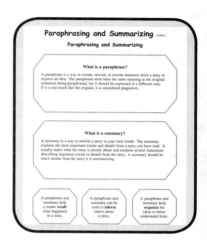

3. Ask volunteers to read aloud the remaining sections of the reference sheet while the rest of the students read along silently. Discuss what summarizing is and how paraphrasing and summarizing help readers recall and organize ideas and inform others of the ideas in a story.

4. Distribute copies of the "Jump Right In!" passage, and display the transparency. Ask volunteers to read assigned portions of the passage while the rest of the students read along silently. Ask the following questions (below and on page 86):

   ✳ What is this story mostly about? (*fishermen who are troubled because they are not catching any fish*)

   ✳ Who are the characters in the story? (*the fishermen and the fish*)

   ✳ What are the characters doing in the story? (*The fishermen are trying to catch some fish but are not happy because they are not catching any; the fish are jumping out of the water and are happy because of the rain.*)

   ✳ What are the important events that occur in the story? (*The fishermen are sitting in their boats and not catching any fish; it starts to rain and they begin to row back to shore; the fish start jumping out of the water; the fish land in the boats.*)

Paraphrasing and Summarizing *(cont.)*

Review *(cont.)*

❋ What are the important details included in the story? (*The fishermen are sad because they are not catching fish; the fish like the rain because it is cool; the fish are excited about the rain; the fishermen are excited about the fish jumping into their boats.*)

Discuss the responses for accuracy. Distribute copies of the "Writing What It's About" handout and display the first page of the transparency. Model how to complete the handout by writing appropriate responses in the shapes labeled "Characters and Their Actions," "Important Events," and "Important Details." Have the students complete these sections on their copy of the handout while you complete them on the transparency. Then continue by asking the following questions:

❋ *Which two sentences would best be paraphrased to be included in the summary?*

❋ What would be a good paraphrase of these sentences?

Discuss the responses, writing each sentence above each line in the shapes labeled "Sentences to Paraphrase" and the paraphrased sentence below the line. Have the students do the same on their copy of the handout.

5. Display the second page of the "Writing What It's About" transparency. With the students' assistance, write a summary of the story on the lines in the box on the transparency, including the two paraphrased sentences. Make sure the students are only helping you write the summary and not copying what you are writing on their handout. After the summary has been written on the transparency, remove the transparency so that it is no longer visible to the students. Tell them to write a summary of the story, including the two paraphrased sentences, and to draw a picture of the summary on their copy of the handout.

6. Ask volunteers to read their summaries. Discuss each summary to make sure it is accurate and includes the paraphrased sentences.

7. Have the students get in pairs. Distribute copies of the "Which Shall She Choose?" passage and sheets of white paper. Tell each pair to read the passage together and discuss the characters, their actions, the important events, and the important details. Have each pair also find two sentences to paraphrase and paraphrase each one. Have the pairs create and complete a graphic organizer (similar to the one on the "Writing What It's About" handout) to show their discussion responses. Then have each member of the pair write his or her own summary, including the two paraphrased sentences, on a sheet of notebook paper.

8. Ask volunteers to read their summaries. Discuss each summary to make sure it is accurate and includes the paraphrased sentences.

Wrap-Up

• To conclude the lesson, ask the following questions: *What is paraphrasing? What is summarizing? What do you need to know to paraphrase and summarize information in a story?*

• Ask volunteers to share their responses. Based on the responses, review what paraphrasing and summarizing are, why they are important, and what needs to be known to paraphrase and summarize.

Paraphrasing and Summarizing *(cont.)*

Paraphrasing and Summarizing

What is a paraphrase?

A paraphrase is a way to restate, reword, or rewrite sentences from a story to express an idea. The paraphrase must have the same meaning as the original sentences being paraphrased, but it should be expressed in a different way. If it is too much like the original, it is considered plagiarism.

What is a summary?

A summary is a way to rewrite a story in your own words. The summary explains the most important events and details from a story you have read. It usually states what the story is mostly about and contains several statements describing important events or details from the story. A summary should be much shorter than the story it is summarizing.

A paraphrase and summary help a reader **recall** what happened in a story.

A paraphrase and summary can be used to **inform** others about a story.

A paraphrase and summary help **organize** the ideas to better understand them.

Paraphrasing and Summarizing (cont.)

Jump Right In!

adapted from the Aesop's fable "The Fisherman and the Tunny-fish"

The fishermen of Baytown were very worried and frustrated at the same time. They had been going out every day to fish but had caught nothing for several weeks. They all sat in their boats with their poles in the water, but nothing was even nibbling on their lines. The fishermen all sat there feeling very dejected and sad. They sat there day after day, but still they came home with nothing.

One day while the fishermen were trying their luck once again, it began raining. The rain came down in droves, causing the fishermen to begin rowing back to shore.

But under the water, the fish were very excited. They had not come up from the bottom of the bay for weeks because the weather above was dry and hot. This made the shallow water very warm and uncomfortable for the fish. However, the cool rain lured them to the top. The fish were so thrilled about the rain that they began jumping out of the water.

This was a mistake, since all the fishermen were heading toward shore. The fish, with thumps and bumps, began landing in the fishermen's boats. The fishermen were overjoyed because of their dumb luck. Now the fishermen had plenty of fish to feed their families. They also had enough to sell at the market.

Paraphrasing and Summarizing *(cont.)*

Writing What It's About

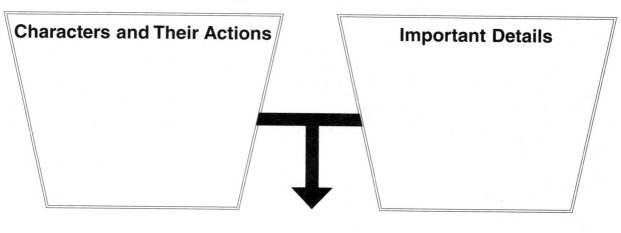

Characters and Their Actions

Important Details

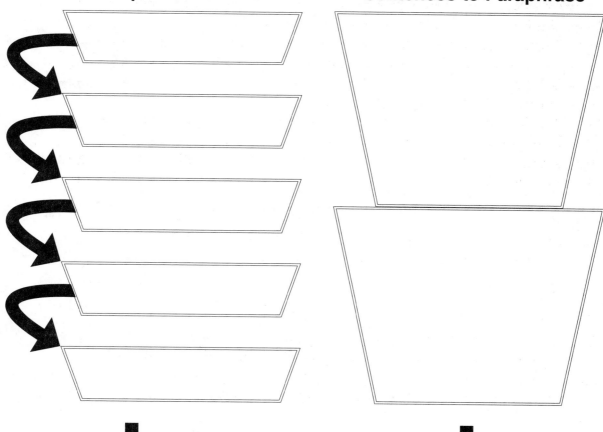

Important Events

Sentences to Paraphrase

Turn to the next page
to paraphrase and summarize

Paraphrasing and Summarizing *(cont.)*

Writing What It's About *(cont.)*

_____

_____

_____

_____

_____

_____

_____

_____

_____

Draw a picture of the story.

Paraphrasing and Summarizing (cont.)

Which Shall She Choose?

adapted from an Asian folktale

There once lived a king who had three sons. His sons were in love with a beautiful princess from a neighboring kingdom. The king told his sons, "Whoever brings the most precious object to me will have the princess's hand in marriage."

So the king's three sons left the kingdom in search of the most precious object. They all traveled in different directions, telling one another they would meet back in one year. The eldest son traveled to a city far to the north. There, he met a merchant selling a small carpet for 40 bags of gold. "Why is this rug so much?" he asked.

"This is a magic rug," replied the merchant. "When you sit on it and tell it where to go, it will instantly transport you to that place."

To test the carpet's magic, the eldest son wished himself to the other side of town. Instantly, he found himself there, so he paid the merchant 40 bags of gold and bought the magic rug.

The middle son of the king traveled south to a city far away. In this city, he met a merchant who was selling a plain ivory tube. He was selling this object for 50 bags of gold. "Why is this ivory tube so much?" asked the middle son.

"This is a magic tube," replied the merchant. "When you look through the tube, you will see any place in the world you wish to see."

The middle son placed the tube to his eye and wished to see his father, the king. Instantly, he saw his father sitting on his throne awaiting the return of his sons. He paid the merchant 50 bags of gold and bought the magic tube.

The youngest son made his journey west over many mountains and great deserts. Finally, he came to a beautiful city far off in the west, touching a large, beautiful sea. In this city, he was met by a merchant who was selling an imitation apple. It was a beautiful wooden apple, but it was not real, and the merchant was selling it for 60 bags of gold. "Why is this wooden apple so much?" asked the youngest son. "What is it about this apple that makes it so expensive?"

"This apple can cure the sick even if they are on death's bed," replied the merchant.

Paraphrasing and Summarizing *(cont.)*

Which Shall She Choose? *(cont.)*

Just as the merchant was finishing his reply, a stranger walked by and said, "My wife is deathly ill. If what you say is true, then let us test the apple on her."

The merchant agreed, and all three men went to the stranger's house. The merchant placed the apple in front of the dying woman's nose, and in a few moments, she was up and cured. After seeing this, the youngest son bought the healing apple.

A year had passed, and the three brothers met on the road about two hundred miles from their father's kingdom. Each showed the magic of the precious object they had purchased. But when the middle son looked through the magic tube, he saw the princess lying in her bed, sick and dying.

"My brothers," he exclaimed. "I see the princess, and she is dying. How can we save her life?"

The youngest brother said, "I can use my healing apple to restore her back to health, but we must get there quickly."

The oldest brother said, "We can use the magic rug to transport ourselves there immediately."

So all three brothers jumped on the magic carpet, and instantly they were in front of the princess's bed. The youngest son placed the healing apple in front of the princess's nose, and in no time she was well again.

But who was to marry her? All the objects were precious, and all had a special gift, so the king left the decision up to the princess.

Since all along she had loved the youngest son, she picked him. But it was not just because she had always loved him; it was because it was the healing apple he brought that saved her life.

Genres

Skill 16: The student will recognize the distinguishing features of genres (e.g., biography, historical fiction, informational texts, poetry).

Instructional Preparation

Materials:

- several examples of each of the following: biographical, historical fiction, informational, and poetry books (*one of each per four-person group*)

Duplicate the following (one per student, unless otherwise indicated):

- "Some Genres and Their Features" reference sheet
- "Recognizing a Passage Type" handout (*one per student pair*)

Prepare a transparency of the following:

- "Some Genres and Their Features" reference sheet
- "In My Dreams!" poem
- "Recognizing a Passage Type" handout

Recall

Before beginning the **Review** component, facilitate a discussion based on the following questions:

- ✳ What is meant by the genre of a passage? (*a particular kind of book or style of writing*)

- ✳ What are some genres of books, passages, or stories you know? (*fiction, nonfiction, poetry, historical fiction, biography, autobiography, informational texts, science fiction, mystery, folktales*)

- ✳ What are the features of a biography? (*Responses will vary.*)

- ✳ What are the features of historical fiction? (*Responses will vary.*)

- ✳ What are the features of an informational text? (*Responses will vary.*)

- ✳ What are the features of poetry? (*Responses will vary.*)

Tell the students that in this lesson they will be reading to practice identifying the specific genre of a passage and describing the features of that genre.

Review

1. Distribute copies of the "Some Genres and Their Features" reference sheet and display the transparency. Ask volunteers to read aloud each section of the reference sheet while the rest of the students read along silently. After each section has been read, discuss the features to make sure the students understand what is meant.

Genres *(cont.)*

Review *(cont.)*

2. Have the students get in four-person groups. Distribute copies of the biographical, historical fiction, informational, and poetry books. Allow the groups to skim through each to look for the different features covered by the discussion of the "Some Genres and Their Features" reference sheet. Then ask for volunteers to share their group's findings.

3. Have the students put away their "Some Genres and Their Features" reference sheet. Display the "In My Dreams!" transparency. Read aloud the passage while the students read along silently. Ask the following questions:

   ✳ What type of genre is this passage? (*poetry*)

   ✳ How do you know this is a poem? (*Responses will vary.*)

   Display the "Some Genres and Their Features" transparency again. Discuss the responses to the above questions, reviewing the important features of poetry on the transparency.

4. Have the students get in pairs. Distribute copies of the "Recognizing a Passage Type" handout and display the transparency. Ask a volunteer to read aloud the "Sister of Mercy" passage while the rest of the students read along silently. Ask the following questions:

   ✳ What type of genre is this passage? (*biography*)

   ✳ How do you know this is a biography? (*Responses will vary.*)

   Discuss the responses, and write the appropriate responses on the transparency in the organizer at the bottom of the "Sister of Mercy" passage. Have the pairs do the same on their copy of the handout. Display again the "Some Genres and Their Features" transparency to review the main features of biographies. Then tell each pair to work together to complete the remaining organizers on the handout. Make sure the students are not using their "Some Genres and Their Features" reference sheet to help them.

5. Ask volunteers to share their responses. Discuss the responses, writing the appropriate responses on the transparency. Display the "Some Genres and Their Features" transparency again to review the main features of each of the remaining genres.

Wrap-Up

- To conclude the lesson, have the students write a response on a sheet of paper to the following prompt: *List the four genres discussed in this lesson. Then describe the major features of each genre.*

- Ask volunteers to share their responses. Discuss the responses for accuracy, using the responses to review how to recognize biographies, historical fiction, informational texts, and poetry, and the features of each one.

Genres (cont.)

Some Genres and Their Features

Biographies

- tells the life story and gives information about a real person

- most often written in time order

- provides information and details that show the person's actions

- shows how the person affected others

- states or implies how the writer feels about the person

Informational Texts

- focuses on a specific idea or subject

- provides information and details about the subject or idea

- supports the subject or idea with facts

- uses explanations, examples, and descriptions to clarify and support ideas

Historical Fiction

- set in a real historical place during a specific period in history

- characters may be real or fictional, but they act in realistic ways

- contains real historical events mixed with fictional ones

- problems/conflicts and dialogue are accurate to the time period

Poetry

- uses rhythm and rhyme

- arranged in lines and stanzas

- uses word pictures to build sensory impressions and create images

- plays with sounds of words and rhythms of phrases

- often uses sensory details and figurative language

- compressed ideas—uses less space and fewer words to convey an idea

Genres (cont.)

In My Dreams!

I once walked

Along a moonlit trail.

I once talked

To a humpback whale

    In my dreams!

I once rang

A golden bell.

I once sang

Like a rock star's yell

    In my dreams!

I can fly in a ship

With a bright green and red alien.

I can slide and slip

With a bunch of hogs in a pigpen.

    In my dreams!

I can run like a cheetah

And growl as loud as many lions.

I can dress like a jester for Mardi Gras

And lie down in a field of dandelions

    In my dreams!

I can be a pirate

Sailing on a great clipper.

I can be an acrobat

Performing a triple flipper

    In my dreams!

I can be an intelligent botanist,

Who grows beautiful rose petals.

I can be a talented gymnast,

Who wins all the gold medals

    In my dreams!

I can be

Anything I want.

I can do

Everything I want

    In my dreams!

Genres *(cont.)*

Recognizing a Passage Type

Sister of Mercy

Mother Teresa was born in 1910. She was born in Skopje, Yugoslavia. At age 12, she knew she wanted to be a missionary. She wished to help people. She joined the Sisters of Loreto at age 18. This order of nuns did missions in India. At age 20, she officially became a nun. She then went to Calcutta. From 1931 to 1948, she taught high school. However, after seeing the suffering in the streets, she left teaching. She left to work with the poor in the slums. In 1950, she started her own order of nuns. The Missionaries of Charity looked after those who were not wanted. Mother Teresa opened many orphanages. She has been given many awards for her work. She died in 1997 still doing what she was called to do: help others.

This passage type is _____

I know this because _____

_____

A Vanishing Act

Dinosaurs died out 65 million years ago. There is still mystery as to why they died. However, dinosaurs weren't the only ones to die. Over half of the world's animals also vanished. There are many reasons why scientists think dinosaurs died off. Many things started to occur during this time. Many volcanoes were erupting. The weather was beginning to change, and the sea levels were rising. There are two main theories why dinosaurs died out. The first is that a giant meteor hit the Earth. This caused dust clouds, acid rain, storms, and huge waves. It changed the climate completely. The second is that erupting volcanoes caused changes in the climate. The one thing that is common between these theories is that both involve changes in the weather—the most likely cause of the dinosaurs dying off.

This passage type is _____

I know this because _____

_____

The Key to Success

Ben Franklin sat in his favorite chair, watching the fierce storm pass over Philadelphia. He studied the lightning as it struck the ground. *I wonder if lightning is an electrical current produced by nature,* he thought to himself. *One of these days I'm going to test that idea.*

So, a few days later, a thunderstorm was expected to occur. Ben decided that hanging a metal key from a kite was the best way to test his idea. When he told Joseph Priestly about his idea, Priestly responded by saying, "Ben Franklin, you would be foolish to try to battle the forces of Mother Nature."

"If lightning is indeed an electrical current," Ben replied, "then I will be under no harm. It will stop once it strikes the key." And with that, Ben went on with his idea.

Once Ben had attached the key to the kite, he began to allow the wind to take the kite high in the sky. He waited and waited. Finally a promising storm cloud was directly over the kite. However, it passed by without letting out one lightning strike. Soon he noticed some pieces of the string standing straight up. Seeing this, Ben gently touched his knuckle against the key, and an electrical spark appeared.

"Hurrah!" Ben yelled. "My theory was accurate. Lightning is electrical current."

And with that, Ben Franklin became the first American to prove the existence of electricity in nature.

This passage type is _____

I know this because _____

_____

_____

Representing Information

Skill 17: The student will represent information from a passage in different ways (e.g., outline, timeline, graphic organizer).

Instructional Preparation

Materials:

- highlighters (*one per student*)
- butcher paper (*one three-foot sheet per three-person group*)
- markers (*one set per three-person group*)

Duplicate the following (one per student, unless otherwise indicated):

- "A Tunnel Built" passage
- "A Timeline" handout
- "A Graphic Organizer: Webbing" handout
- "Built Across Land" passage

Prepare a transparency of the following:

- "A Tunnel Built" passage
- "A Timeline" handout
- "A Graphic Organizer: Webbing" handout

Recall

Before beginning the **Review** component, facilitate a discussion based on the following questions:

* What are different ways you can show information from a passage you've read? (*by writing key words and phrases from the passage in the form of an outline that shows the important information; by sequencing the important events in the passage in order on a timeline; by creating a graphic organizer to show the important details in the passage; by writing key words and phrases in the form of a list of notes*)

* How is an outline constructed? (*by using Roman numerals, capital letters, numbers, and lower-case letters to organize the information in sections*)

* How is a timeline constructed? (*by writing the important dates along a line containing hash marks and describing what occurred on those dates*)

* How is a graphic organizer constructed? (*by writing important information and details on a graphical image that ties it all together*)

* Why is it important to show information from a passage in different forms, including an outline, a timeline, and a graphic organizer? (*It places information into a form that is easier to understand and read; it shows that the reader understands which information in the passage is important and which is not.*)

Tell the students that in this review lesson they will be reading several passages and will transfer the information and represent it in outline, timeline, and graphic-organizer formats.

Representing Information *(cont.)*

Review

1. Distribute copies of the "A Tunnel Built" passage and display the transparency. Read aloud the passage while the students read it silently. Distribute the highlighters. With the students' assistance, reread through each paragraph of the passage, identifying the most important information. Underline the important information on the transparency while the students highlight it on their copy of the handout.

2. On a sheet of chart paper, model, with the students' assistance, how to create and complete an outline of the important information in the "A Tunnel Built" passage. (Use the answer key on page 174 to help you complete the outline.) Have the students create and complete an outline on a sheet of notebook paper while you make one on the chart paper. Discuss the outline to make sure the students understand its purpose and how to create and complete one.

3. Distribute copies of the "A Timeline" handout and display the transparency. Model how to complete the handout. Have the students complete their copy of the handout while you complete it on the transparency. Follow a similar procedure to show how to complete the "A Graphic Organizer: Webbing" handout. Discuss the timeline and graphic organizer to make sure the students understand their purposes and how to create and complete each one.

4. Distribute copies of the "Built Across Land" passage. Have the students read it silently and highlight the important information. Tell the students to get in three-person groups. Have each group discuss the passage to come to a consensus regarding the most important information that should be highlighted.

5. Distribute the butcher paper and markers. Assign each group a number—1, 2, or 3. Using the butcher paper, have the groups with number 1 create an outline, those with number 2 create a timeline, and those with number 3 create a graphic organizer based on the important information highlighted in the passage.

6. Have each group present its outline, timeline, or graphic organizer. Discuss each one to determine if the information on it is accurate and effective.

Wrap-Up

- To conclude the lesson, pose the following questions: *What is an outline, and what is it used for? What is a timeline, and what is it used for? What is a graphic organizer, and what is it used for? Why is it important to show information from a passage in different ways?*

- Ask volunteers to share their thoughts. Use the responses as an opportunity to review how to represent information in a passage in the form of an outline, a timeline, or a graphic organizer.

Representing Information *(cont.)*

A Tunnel Built

In the late 1800s, the car was invented. It grew in popularity. Many people had one. The car allowed people to get around faster. But people in New York City and New Jersey wanted to get back and forth more quickly. They wanted some way to cross the Hudson River. The Hudson runs between New York City and New Jersey. In 1906, a commission made up of people from these two places was set up. They wanted to look into building a bridge across the Hudson. But that was turned down. It would be much too costly. It was decided to build a tunnel beneath the Hudson. A tunnel would be less affected by weather.

The project to build the tunnel was called the "Hudson River Vehicular Tunnel Project." In 1919, Clifford Holland was chosen to lead the project. Construction began in 1920. The biggest challenge was getting air into the tunnel. The fear was that fumes from cars would be harmful. These fumes would affect those traveling in the tunnel. So engineers came up with a plan. They built an automatic ventilation system. This system would make the air cleaner in the tunnel. It would actually be purer than the air above ground. This tunnel was the first of its kind. It was the first fixed vehicle crossing from New York City to New Jersey. It was also the first mechanically ventilated vehicle tunnel.

Two tunnels were dug: one from New Jersey and one from New York City. The work was difficult. In 1924, tragedy struck the project. Holland passed away. He died one day before the two tunnels were to link up. But construction continued.

Finally, in 1927, the tunnel opened. It was named the Holland Tunnel. The name came from its first chief engineer, Clifford Holland. The toll for the tunnel was 50 cents. It was about one-and-one-half miles long. It took eight minutes to pass through. On the first day, 51,694 vehicles passed through. The Holland Tunnel cost about $50 million to build. Today it would cost over $1.4 billion. The tunnel is still used. Since it was built, over 1.3 billion vehicles have used the tunnel.

Representing Information *(cont.)*

A Timeline

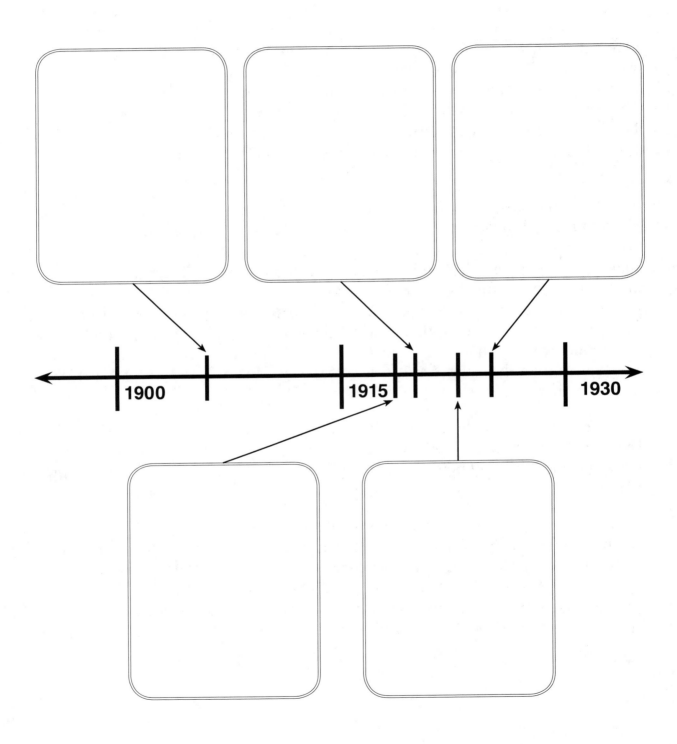

Representing Information *(cont.)*

A Graphic Organizer: Webbing

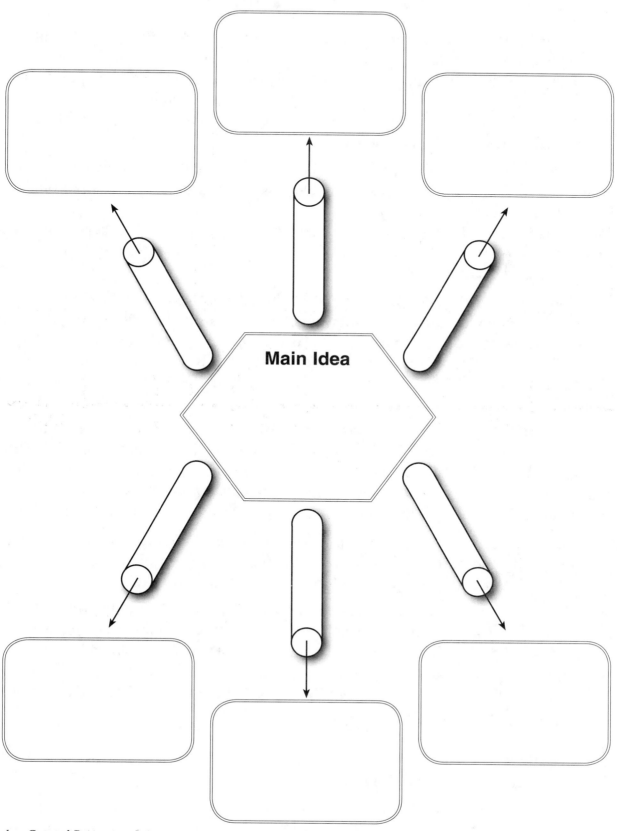

Main Idea

Built Across Land

For centuries, sailing from the Pacific Ocean to the Atlantic was difficult. It took many months to do this. Sailors from around the world wanted to build a canal across Panama. This would make sailing between these oceans quicker and easier. Since part of Panama was only 40 miles across, it was the best choice. Finally, between 1904 and 1914, the United States built the canal. The dream of many sailors had come true.

The Panama Canal cuts across the Isthmus[1] of Panama. It allows ships to travel between the Pacific and Atlantic Oceans. This waterway passes through Panama. It stretches across 40 miles of hilly terrain. It is made up of man-made lakes, channels, and a series of locks. Locks are water-filled chambers. These chambers help raise and lower ships over the land. But how did the Panama Canal come to get built?

For many years, many people in the United States had wanted to build a canal. They wanted to build it somewhere across Central America. They looked at both Nicaragua and Panama. But it was thought that Panama was the better place. So in 1902, Congress and President Theodore Roosevelt decided to build the Panama Canal. They signed a treaty with Columbia. At the time, Panama was under Columbian rule. But the treaty was rejected.

Panama really wanted the canal built in its country. So in 1903, Panama declared its independence. It no longer wanted to be under Columbian rule. The United States supported the revolt. Soon after, the United States signed a treaty with Panama. This gave the United States Panama's consent to build the canal. The United States bought a strip of land. Now it was ready to build the canal.

Construction on the canal began in 1904. Independent contractors did most of the digging and building. In all, 100,000 people moved to Panama. They moved there from all over. They did this so they could work on the canal.

The Panama Canal was completed in 1914. The first ship sailed through on August 15. But in 1915, the canal was closed. It was shut down because of landslides. The canal had become too dangerous. Then World War I began. This delayed the official opening of the canal for over five years. The canal was officially opened in 1920. Since its opening, the Panamal Canal has served ships from all over the world.

---

[1] *a narrow piece of land with sea on both sides*

Text Organizers

Skill 18: The student will use text organizers (e.g., headings, graphic features, tables of contents) to locate and organize information.

Instructional Preparation

Duplicate the following (one per student, unless otherwise indicated):

- "Text Organizers" reference sheet
- "Interesting Animals" passage
- "Locate and Organize" handout
- "Animals of the World" passage (*one per student pair*)
- "Locate and Organize the Thorny Devil" handout (*one per student pair*)

Prepare a transparency of the following:

- "Text Organizers" reference sheet
- "Interesting Animals" passage
- "Locate and Organize" handout
- "Locate and Organize the Thorny Devil" handout

Recall

Before beginning the **Review** component, facilitate a discussion based on the following questions:

❋ What strategies can a reader use to locate and organize information? (*look at the headings; look at the pictures or maps; look at the table of contents; carefully read the information under each heading*)

❋ What is a heading? (*a word or phrase that indicates what the following paragraph or paragraphs will be about*)

❋ What kinds of graphic features do you know? (*maps, graphs, pictures, charts, etc.*)

❋ What is a table of contents? (*the listing of chapter titles at the front of a book*)

❋ Why might it be important to locate and organize information? (*to find a specific piece of information; to be sure that the information is understood*)

Review

1. Distribute copies of the "Text Organizers" reference sheet and display the transparency. Ask volunteers to read the information in each box. Facilitate a discussion about the different ways to locate and organize information.

2. Distribute copies of the "Interesting Animals" passage and display the transparency. Read the information in the table of contents box aloud while the students read along silently. Then ask the following question:

   - How can the table of contents help you locate information? (*The chapters' titles give hints as to what topic each chapter is about.*)

Text Organizers *(cont.)*

Review *(cont.)*

3. Read the "Two Lizards" passage aloud while the students read along silently. Then ask the following questions:

   ✳ How can the maps in the passage help you locate information? (*The maps give additional information about the topic; the maps clarify information in the passage; the maps give graphic information on where something or someone is located.*)

   ✳ How can the headings in the passage help you locate and organize the information? (*They indicate the topics in the passage that can be used in a graphic organizer; they help you locate specific information.*)

4. Distribute copies of the "Locate and Organize" handout and display the transparency. Ask the following questions:

   ✳ In which chapter would you learn about anoles and basilisks? (*chapter 4*)

   ✳ How did you locate this information? (*by looking at the chapter titles in the table of contents*)

   ✳ Where are the most anoles found in the United States? (*Florida*)

   ✳ How did you locate this information? (*by looking at the U.S. map and reading the caption*)

   ✳ On which continent can basilisks be found? (*South America*)

   ✳ How did you locate this information? (*by looking at the map and the caption at the beginning of the passage*)

   Record accurate responses in the appropriate spaces on the transparency and have the students do the same on their copy of the handout.

5. Have the students look at the web in the "Organizing Information" section of the handout. Point out that the title of the passage ("Two Lizards") is in the top box and that the headings found in the passage ("Basilisks" and "Anoles") are in the next two boxes. Ask volunteers to determine the information that should go in the "Live," "Color," "Length," and "Eat" boxes. Record appropriate responses on the transparency and have students do the same on their copy of the handout.

6. Have the students pair up. Distribute copies of the "Animals of the World" passage. Read the table of contents and the passage aloud while the students read along silently.

7. Distribute copies of the "Locate and Organize the Thorny Devil" handout. Have the students complete the handout according to the directions.

8. When the students have finished, display the "Locate and Organize the Thorny Devil" transparency. Ask volunteers to share their responses. Discuss each response for accuracy.

Wrap-Up

- To conclude the review, have the students use the reverse side of their "Text Organizers" reference sheet to respond to the following questions: *How can a reader use the table of contents, graphic features, and headings to locate information? How can a reader use the headings in a passage to help organize the information?*

- After the students have finished, ask volunteers to share their responses. Use the responses as a means to review how tables of contents, graphic features, and headings can help a reader locate and organize information.

Text Organizers *(cont.)*

Text Organizers

Books and passages are organized to help you understand their meaning. The ways in which books and passages are organized can help a reader locate and organize information. Tables of contents, graphic features, and headings are three methods used to help a reader locate and organize information in books and passages.

Tables of Contents

Tables of contents are found at the beginning of the books, and they help the reader locate information.

Graphic Features

Graphic features such as pictures and maps help the reader locate information in a passage.

Headings

Headings help the reader locate and organize information in a passage.

Text Organizers *(cont.)*

Interesting Animals

Interesting Animals	
Table of Contents	
Chapter	Title
1	Beautiful Birds
2	Cool Cats
3	Interesting Insects
4	Likable Lizards
5	Special Spiders

Two Lizards

There are many kinds of lizards in the world, and two of these are the basilisk and the anole.

Basilisks

These lizards live in trees and rocks near the water. They live in tropical areas. The most amazing thing about these lizards is that they can run on water for a short time. Their legs and their tail help them achieve this. Their back feet have special scales that also help them run on water. Basilisks are green or brown in color. They are 2 to 2½ feet long and eat insects, spiders, and worms.

Basilisks are found in the tropical rain forests of South America.

Anoles

There are two kinds of this lizard: the green anole and the brown anole. They like to live in tropical areas and can be found in the southeastern part of the United States. Anoles are found in bushes, trees, and on rock walls and houses. They like to sit in the warm sun. Anoles can be up to 9 inches long and like to eat insects and spiders.

In the United States, you can find the most anoles in Florida.

Text Organizers *(cont.)*

Locate and Organize

Locating Information

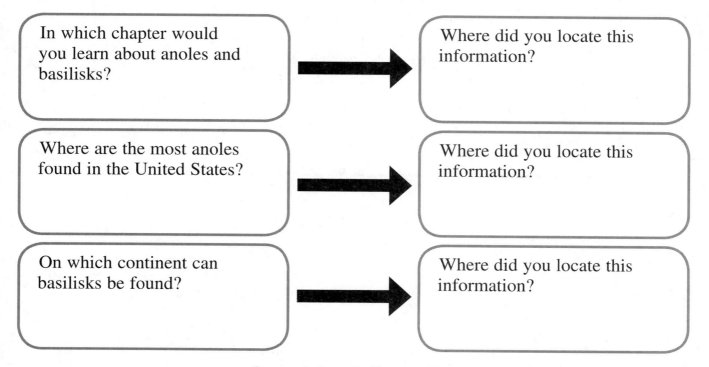

In which chapter would you learn about anoles and basilisks? → Where did you locate this information?

Where are the most anoles found in the United States? → Where did you locate this information?

On which continent can basilisks be found? → Where did you locate this information?

Organizing Information

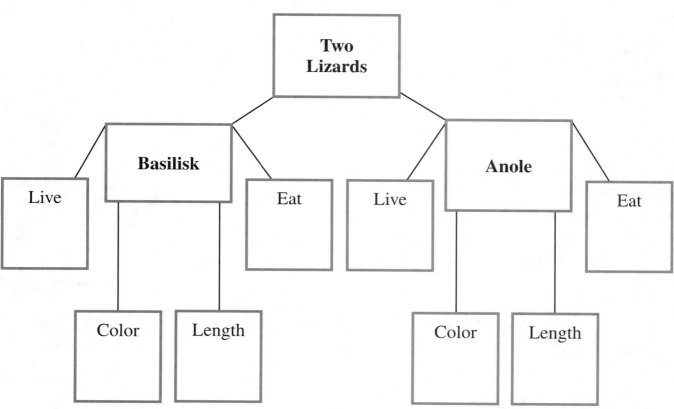

Two Lizards

Basilisk — Live, Eat, Color, Length

Anole — Live, Eat, Color, Length

Text Organizers (cont.)

Animals of the World

The Thorny Devil

Thorny devils are found throughout inland Australia.

Where they live

Thorny devils can be found in Australia. They like areas that are sandy but they also can be found in rocky areas.

What they look like

As their name suggests, thorny devils have thorny spines. These spines are used for protection. Thorny devils can change color. When they are warm and active, they are yellow and red. When they are frightened or cold, they are a dark olive color. Female thorny devils are usually bigger than the males. Females can be more than four inches long. Males are usually under four inches long.

What they eat

Thorny devils like to eat one thing: ants. These lizards can eat up to 45 ants in one minute. In one meal, a thorny devil may eat up to 2,500 ants.

Other Things a Thorny Devil Might Eat
stones
sticks
tiny insect eggs

What they do

Thorny devils move very little during the coldest winter months and the hottest summer months. But when they do move, they walk slowly. Sometimes they freeze in place. This is a way of protecting themselves.

Text Organizers *(cont.)*

Locate and Organize the Thorny Devil

Directions: Answer the questions in the "Locate" section. Then create a web similar to the one on the "Locate and Organize" handout in the "Organize" section to organize the information in "The Thorny Devil" passage.

Locate

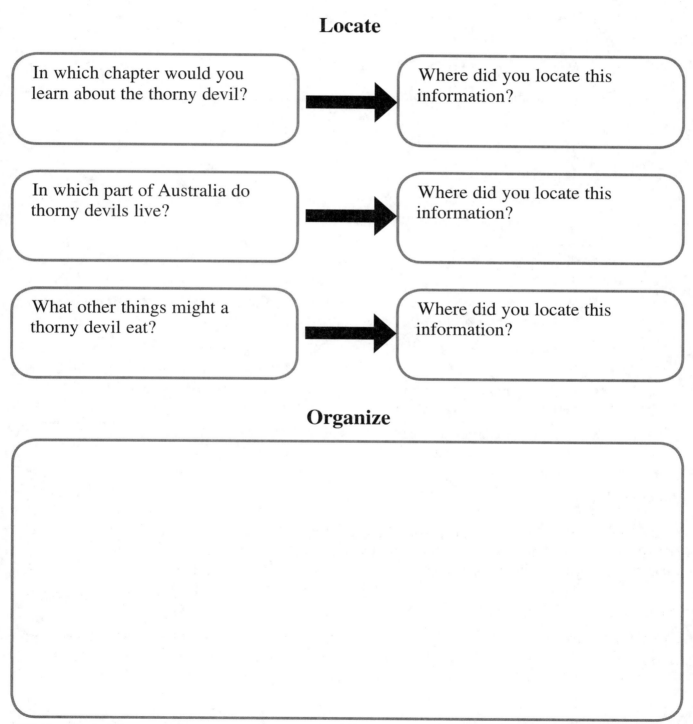

In which chapter would you learn about the thorny devil? → Where did you locate this information?

In which part of Australia do thorny devils live? → Where did you locate this information?

What other things might a thorny devil eat? → Where did you locate this information?

Organize

Subject-Verb Agreement

Skill 19: The student will demonstrate an understanding of the appropriate usage of subject-verb agreement.

Instructional Preparation

Duplicate the following (one per student, unless otherwise indicated):

- "Subject-Verb Agreement" reference sheet
- "The Basic Rules" reference sheet
- "Make Them Agree" handout
- "More Agreement Practice" handout

Prepare a transparency of the following:

- "Subject-Verb Agreement" reference sheet
- "The Basic Rules" reference sheet
- "Make Them Agree" handout
- "More Agreement Practice" handout

Recall

Before beginning the **Review** component, facilitate a discussion based on the following questions:

* What is meant by a subject's "number" or a verb's "number"? (*whether the subject or verb is singular or plural*)

* When a subject and a verb have the same number in a sentence, what is this called? (*subject-verb agreement*)

* Why is it important that every sentence have a subject that agrees in number with the verb? (*Sentences without subject-verb agreement are not correctly written.*)

* Why is it important to learn the rules of subject-verb agreement? (*so that a student's writing can improve; so that a student can write a correct sentence*)

Review

1. To begin instruction, distribute copies of the "Subject-Verb Agreement" reference sheet and display the first page of the transparency. Read the page aloud while the students read it silently. Discuss what agreeing in number means and give examples.

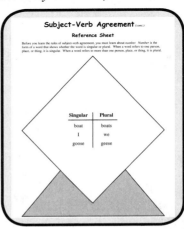

Subject-Verb Agreement *(cont.)*

Review *(cont.)*

2. Display "The Basic Rules" reference sheet and ask a volunteer to read the first rule and example sentence. Discuss the rule after it has been read. Ask another volunteer to write on the classroom board an original sentence that follows the rule. Examine the sentence with the class to check for accuracy in regard to the rule. Continue this procedure for each of the remaining rules on the reference sheet. After reading the first two rules, point out that singular and plural verbs are different from singular and plural nouns. Tell the students that singular verbs have an *s* or *es* added to them, much as plural nouns have an *s* or *es* added to them. Explain that plural verbs do not have an *s* or *es* added to them, just as singular nouns do not have an *s* or *es* added to them.

3. Have the students get into three-person groups. Distribute copies of the "Make Them Agree" handout. Have the students read the sentences and circle the verb that correctly completes the sentence. The students may discuss each sentence with the group and may refer to the reference sheets, but each student is responsible for completing his or her copy of the handout.

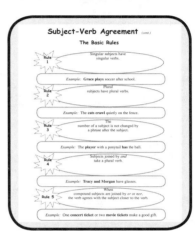

4. Display the "Make Them Agree" transparency. Ask a volunteer to read the first sentence aloud while inserting the correct verb. Ask another volunteer to indicate which subject-verb agreement rule the sentence follows. Discuss why the sentence follows the indicated rule and circle the correct answer on the transparency. Continue this procedure for the remaining sentences.

5. Distribute copies of the "More Agreement Practice" handout. Tell the students that they are going to examine several more sentences to practice using correct subject-verb agreement. Have them follow the directions and complete the handout.

6. Display the "More Agreement Practice" transparency. Ask volunteers to read each sentence aloud while inserting the correct verb and to indicate which rule the sentence follows. Discuss each sentence and rule for accuracy. Write the appropriate responses on the transparency.

Wrap-Up

- To conclude this lesson, have the students use the reverse side of their "More Agreement Practice" handout to respond to the following prompts: *Describe what subject-verb agreement means. Then, using three different rules, write three sentences that show proper subject-verb agreement.*

- Ask several volunteers to read their responses and sentences aloud. Facilitate a discussion that uses the responses to emphasize the rules of subject-verb agreement.

Subject-Verb Agreement *(cont.)*

Reference Sheet

Before you learn the rules of subject-verb agreement, you must learn about *number.* *Number* is the form of a word that shows whether the word is singular or plural. When a word refers to one person, place, or thing, it is singular. When a word refers to more than one person, place, or thing, it is plural.

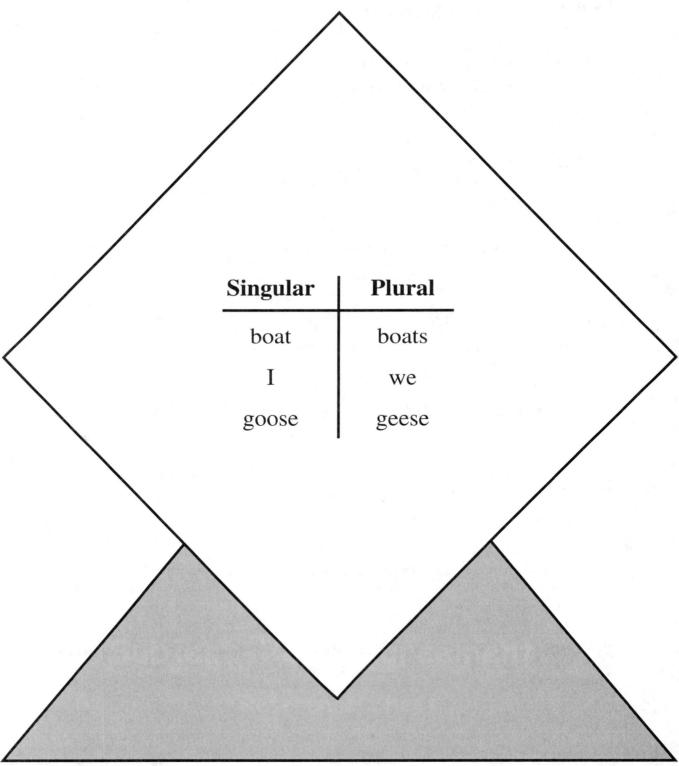

Singular	Plural
boat	boats
I	we
goose	geese

Subject-Verb Agreement *(cont.)*

The Basic Rules

Rule 1

Singular subjects have singular verbs.

Example: **Grace plays** soccer after school.

Rule 2

Plural subjects have plural verbs.

Example: The **cats crawl** quietly on the fence.

Rule 3

The number of a subject is not changed by a phrase after the subject.

Example: The **player** with a ponytail **has** the ball.

Rule 4

Subjects joined by *and* take a plural verb.

Example: **Tracy and Morgan** have glasses.

Rule 5

When compound subjects are joined by *or* or *nor*, the verb agrees with the subject closer to the verb.

Example: One **concert ticket** or two **movie tickets** make a good gift.

Subject-Verb Agreement *(cont.)*

Make Them Agree

Directions: Circle the correct verb to use in each sentence. Rewrite the sentence on the line provided.

1. The boys (**wear**, **wears**) ties.

   _____

2. The cat with a spot on its head (**sleeps**, **sleep**) on top of the refrigerator.

   _____

3. The teachers, the parents, and the students (**talks**, **talk**) with the principal.

   _____

4. Neither the blue sweater nor the red sweater (**fits**, **fit**).

   _____

5. Leslie and Jenny (**enjoy**, **enjoys**) baking cookies.

   _____

6. Carlos (**like**, **likes**) to draw pictures.

   _____

7. The mayor of the city (**are**, **is**) unable to come to the grand opening.

   _____

8. The cupcakes at the bake sale (**were**, **was**) all sold.

   _____

9. Mario (**clean**, **cleans**) his desk.

   _____

10. Two quarters or one token (**buy**, **buys**) a bus ticket.

    _____

Subject-Verb Agreement *(cont.)*

More Agreement Practice

Directions: Complete each of these sentences using the appropriate verb. The verbs are below the blank line in each sentence. Then write the number of the rule that the sentence follows on the blank line in the box next to the sentence.

1. Jake, Roland, and Juan _____ to school together. *(walk/walks)*

   Rule _____

2. The smallest kitten in the litter _____ on the fence. *(jumps/jump)*

   Rule _____

3. Neither he nor they _____ invited to the party. *(is/are)*

   Rule _____

4. The girls _____ on new dresses for the dance. *(tries/try)*

   Rule _____

5. Ashley _____ to be an actress. *(pretend/pretends)*

   Rule _____

6. Mary _____ her breakfast. *(eat/eats)*

   Rule _____

7. Tom, George, and Mike _____ in the mountains. *(hike/hikes)*

   Rule _____

8. The boys _____ to the movies. *(goes/go)*

   Rule _____

Adjectives and Adverbs

Skill 20: The student will use adjectives and adverbs.

Instructional Preparation

Materials:
- a large, round ball

Duplicate the following (one per student, unless otherwise indicated):
- "Adjectives and Adverbs" reference sheet
- "Using Adjectives" handout
- "Using Adverbs" handoutK

Prepare a transparency of the following:
- "Adjectives and Adverbs" reference sheet
- "Using Adjectives" handout
- "Using Adverbs" handout

Recall

Before beginning the **Review** component, facilitate a discussion based on these questions:

✳ What is an adjective? (*a word that describes a noun or pronoun*)

✳ Why do we use adjectives? (*to more vividly and expressively describe nouns or pronouns in a sentence or while writing a passage*)

✳ What is an adverb? (*a word that describes a verb, adjective, or another adverb*)

✳ Why do we use adverbs? (*to more thoroughly describe an action that is occurring in a sentence or a passage*)

Review

1. Show the ball to the students. Ask volunteers to describe the ball using one-word responses, making sure the students use adjectives to describe the ball. Assign another volunteer to write the students' responses on the classroom board under the heading "This Ball." After an adequate number of responses have been recorded, explain about using adjectives to vividly describe objects, people, places, things, and ideas (nouns).

2. After adequately discussing the use of adjectives to help describe nouns, throw the ball softly to a student. Ask the following question:

   ✳ What did I just do with the ball? (*threw it*)

   Continue asking the following questions, making sure the students respond using adverbs.

   ✳ How did I throw it? (*softly, easily, gently*)

   ✳ When did I throw it? (*recently, just now, a moment ago*)

   ✳ Where did I throw it? (*over there, inside, somewhere, nearby*)

Adjectives and Adverbs *(cont.)*

Review *(cont.)*

Discuss the responses. Ask a volunteer to record the adverbs on the classroom board under the heading "Threw the Ball." Continue the procedure by rolling or bouncing the ball and asking the "How," "When," and "Where" questions. Then discuss the use of adverbs to help describe actions.

3. Distribute copies of the "Adjectives and Adverbs" reference sheet, and display the transparency. Ask volunteers to read aloud assigned sections of the reference sheet while the rest of the students read along silently. Discuss the rules of adjective and adverb usage, and ask volunteers to share further examples of each rule.

4. Write the following words on the classroom board: *grateful, helpful, impatiently, playfully.* Then, below the words, write the following sentences:

   • This was the most _____ my sister had ever been in cleaning the house.

   • He _____ waited for his sister to finish her homework.

   Read aloud the first sentence while the students read along silently. Ask the following questions, reminding the students to consider the comparative and superlative forms of the words on the board when needed:

   ✳ Which word from the list would you use to complete this sentence? (*helpful*)

   ✳ Why do you think that? (*The sentence is making a comparison about how helpful the sister has been compared with all other times when cleaning the house.*)

   Write the appropriate words on the blank line of the first sentence. Then continue, using this procedure with the next question.

5. Tell the students they will be reading sentences and selecting the correct adjective or adverb to complete the sentence. Distribute copies of the "Using Adjectives" handout and display the transparency. Read the directions aloud while the students read them silently. Work through the first few sentences with the students to model how to complete the handout. Then distribute copies of the "Using Adverbs" handout. Tell the students the procedure is the same for completing this handout. Have the students complete each handout independently.

6. Ask volunteers to tell how they completed the sentences. Discuss the responses, then write the appropriate words to complete each sentence on the "Using Adjectives" and the "Using Adverbs" transparencies.

Wrap-Up

• To conclude the lesson, have the students write a response on a sheet of notebook paper to the following prompt: *Write four sentences using adjectives and adverbs correctly.*

• Ask volunteers to share their sentences by writing them on the classroom board. Discuss the sentences to make sure the adjectives and adverbs have been used correctly. Use the discussion as a means to review how to use adjectives and adverbs correctly in a sentence.

Adjectives and Adverbs (cont.)

Adjectives and Adverbs

An **adjective** is a word that describes a noun or pronoun. It tells what kind and how many.

Comparative adjectives

- Compare two people, places, things, or ideas
- Add *er* to the end of one-syllable adjectives
- Add *more* before adjectives with two or more syllables
- *Examples:* quick ⟶ quicker   humorous ⟶ more humorous

Superlative adjectives

- Compare three or more people, places, things, or ideas
- Add *est* to the end of one-syllable adjectives
- Add *most* before adjectives with two or more syllables
- *Examples:* quick ⟶ quickest   humorous ⟶ most humorous

Comparative and superlative adjectives

- Change the *y* to an *i* when adding *er* or *est* to the end of an adjective that ends with a consonant and *y*.
- *Example:* lucky ⟶ luckier ⟶ luckiest

An **adverb** is a word that describes a verb, adjective, or another adverb. It tells how, when, or where an action takes place.

Comparative adverbs

- Add *er* to the end of one-syllable adverbs
- Add *more* or *less* before adverbs with two or more syllables
- *Examples:* straight ⟶ straighter   skillfully ⟶ more skillfully

Superlative adverbs

- Add *est* to the end of one-syllable adverbs
- Add *most* or *least* before adverbs with two or more syllables
- *Examples:* straight ⟶ straightest   skillfully ⟶ least skillfully

Adjectives and Adverbs *(cont.)*

Using Adjectives

Directions: Use the words in the Word Bank to complete each sentence. Use the comparative and superlative forms of these words when needed.

Word Bank			
cheerful	crazy	golden	handsome
gleaming	gloomy	necessary	nervous
million	dozen	dreadful	uneasy

1. Kent bought a _____ roses to give to his mom for her birthday.

2. Because of the rain, they had the _____ time at the party.

3. Hershel had the _____ idea about jumping off the bridge into Snake River.

4. Macy was _____ than Anita about the dance recital.

5. The star of the show was even _____ than I had imagined.

6. This was the _____ I had seen my father in days.

7. It seemed as if the mountains were a _____ miles away.

8. After the race ended, Tyrone had the _____ look on his face.

9. The _____ sunlight shone upon the water like _____ diamonds.

10. We had an _____ feeling about going into the _____ cave.

Name: _____

Adjectives and Adverbs *(cont.)*

Using Adverbs

Directions: Use the words in the Word Bank to complete each sentence. Use the comparative and superlative forms of these words when needed.

> **Word Bank**
>
> | afterward | awkwardly | nearby | peacefully |
> |-----------|-----------|-----------|------------|
> | gradually | immediately | underneath | finally |
> | regularly | curiously | especially | recently |

1. Frederick's parents left the key _____ the front-door mat.

2. My best friend, Felix, lives _____ , so we should go see him.

3. _____ after the game, we went to the ice cream shop.

4. The monkey _____ lifted the coconut off the ground.

5. She _____ grabbed hold of the mug before it fell.

6. Veronica _____ moved the bed to where she wanted it.

7. The school had _____ thrown a carnival to raise money for field trips.

8. He slept _____ today than yesterday since the wind had _____ died down.

9. Meryl finally got a job at the bookstore after _____ shopping there over the past year.

10. I think she _____ liked the chocolate-covered strawberries.

Capitalization

Skill 21: The student will use correct capitalization (e.g., names of languages, nationalities).

Instructional Preparation

Duplicate the following (one per student, unless otherwise indicated):

- "Correct Capitalization" reference sheet
- "Your Turn to Capitalize" handout

Prepare a transparency of the following:

- "Correct Capitalization" reference sheet
- "Let's Capitalize!" sheet
- "Your Turn to Capitalize" handout

Recall

Before beginning the **Review** component, facilitate a discussion based on the following questions:

✳ Which kinds of words do we capitalize when we write? (*the first word in a sentence; names; days of the week; days of the month*)

✳ Why do we capitalize certain types of words when we write? (*capital letters provide important visual clues that make reading easier*)

✳ What might happen if we did not use capital letters where they are necessary? (*The reader might confuse the meaning of a sentence or paragraph.*)

Tell the students that in today's lesson they will learn some capitalization rules and practice capitalizing correctly.

Review

1. Distribute copies of the "Correct Capitalization" reference sheet and display the transparency. Ask volunteers to read the two rules of capitalization provided on the reference sheet. After each rule has been read, ask additional volunteers to write sentences on the classroom board that require capitalization of languages and/or nationalities.

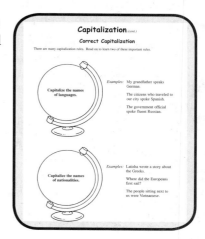

Capitalization *(cont.)*

Review *(cont.)*

2. Display the "Let's Capitalize!" transparency. Ask a volunteer to read the first sentence aloud while the rest of the students read it silently. Ask the following questions:

   ✳ Which word in the sentence is not capitalized correctly? (*Spanish*)

   ✳ How do you know this? (*Spanish is a language, so it should be capitalized because we always capitalize names of languages.*)

   Discuss the responses. Ask a volunteer to come to the overhead projector and cross out the word that is not capitalized correctly and write the correct one above it. Continue this procedure with the remaining sentences on the transparency. Some of the sentences do not contain any errors. For those, write "correct as is" above each one.

3. Have the students get into groups of three. Distribute the "Your Turn to Capitalize" handout and display the transparency. Have each group work together to complete the handout by reading each sentence and then rewriting it using correct capitalization. Remind the students that each member of the group is responsible for completing his or her handout.

4. Ask volunteers to rewrite the sentences correctly on the transparency. Have the other students check the rewritten sentences for accuracy.

Wrap-Up

• To conclude this lesson, have the students use the reverse side of their "Your Turn to Capitalize" handout to respond to the following prompt: *Write two sentences. One sentence should use the capitalization of languages correctly, and the other sentence should use the capitalization of nationalities correctly.*

• Ask several volunteers to write their sentences on the classroom board. Check each sentence for accuracy. Use the sentences to review the main points for capitalizing languages and nationalities.

Capitalization *(cont.)*

Correct Capitalization

There are many capitalization rules. Read on to learn two of these important rules.

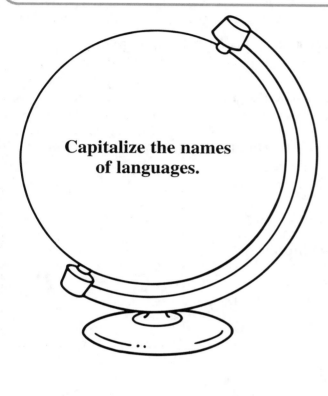

Capitalize the names of languages.

Examples: My grandfather speaks German.

The citizens who traveled to our city spoke Spanish.

The government official spoke fluent Russian.

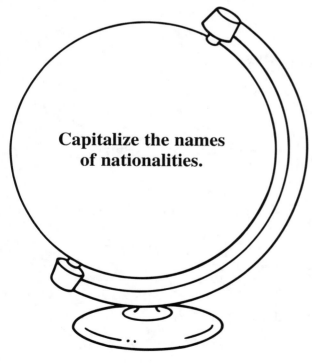

Capitalize the names of nationalities.

Examples: Latisha wrote a story about the Greeks.

Where did the Europeans first sail?

The people sitting next to us were Vietnamese.

Capitalization *(cont.)*

Let's Capitalize!

1. Mary and Joe spoke spanish to each other during lunch.

2. One of the requirements for graduation is to take a Foreign Language class.

3. The children down the street know finnish and english.

4. Jesse taught himself how to read and write in German.

5. What languages do your parents know?

6. I hope to take a course in latin when I start high school.

7. The gymnasts were Russian and they always did well.

8. What nationality do you think that man is?

9. My father is mexican.

10. The dancers were polynesian and wore grass skirts.

11. Learning how to speak japanese is difficult.

12. There are many different Nationalities in the world.

13. The exchange student was belgian and spoke english and french.

14. I had Thai food for the first time last night.

15. There are many different Languages that are african.

Capitalization *(cont.)*

Your Turn to Capitalize

1. A good second language to learn is spanish.

_____

_____

2. Her nationality is peruvian.

_____

_____

3. We learned about some of the romans in our history class.

_____

_____

4. If you want to learn chinese, you will need to study harder.

_____

_____

5. Her native language is farsi, not english.

_____

_____

6. She comes from irish, german, and swedish descent.

_____

_____

7. Some of her ancestors are british subjects.

_____

_____

8. I learned how to speak italian while in college.

_____

_____

Punctuation

Skill 22: The student will use correct punctuation (e.g., commas in a series, commas in direct address, commas and quotation marks in dialogue, apostrophes in possessives).

Instructional Preparation

Materials:

- red or purple pen or pencil (*one per student*)

Duplicate the following (one per student, unless otherwise indicated):

- "Some Rules of Punctuation" reference sheet
- "Punctuate It and Rewrite It!" handout

Prepare a transparency of the following:

- "It's All about Punctuation" sentence list
- "Some Rules of Punctuation" reference sheet
- "Punctuate It and Rewrite It!" handout

Recall

Before beginning the **Review** component, facilitate a discussion based on the following questions:

- ✳ When should you use commas when writing? (*in words in a series; in direct address; in dialogue; to separate adjectives; to set off appositives; between independent clauses*)

- ✳ When should you use quotation marks when writing? (*to show someone is speaking; to show the title of a poem or song*)

- ✳ When should you use apostrophes when writing? (*to form possessives; to form contractions*)

- ✳ Why is it important to use commas, quotation marks, and apostrophes when writing? (*Commas keep words and ideas from running together; commas tell a reader where to pause; quotation marks show when dialogue is happening among two or more people or characters; apostrophes help show when an object or idea belongs to a specific person; they make your writing easier to read.*)

Tell the students that in this review lesson they will be applying some rules for commas, quotation marks, and apostrophes to correctly use these forms of punctuation in a sentence.

Review

1. Display the "It's All about Punctuation" transparency. Read the first sentence aloud as the students read along silently. Make sure to pause as if commas were present in the sentence. Ask the following questions (below and on pge 129):

   - ✳ What is incorrect about this sentence? (*It is missing several commas.*)

Punctuation *(cont.)*

Review *(cont.)*

✳ How would you correct the mistakes? (*Place commas after the words "cold" and "dark."*)

Discuss the responses, and correct the sentence by placing commas in their appropriate places. Ask a volunteer to come to the overhead and correctly rewrite the sentence below the original sentence. Continue this questioning procedure with the remaining sentences on the transparency.

2. Distribute copies of the "Some Rules of Punctuation" reference sheet and display the transparency. Ask volunteers to read aloud each rule on the reference sheet while the rest of the students read silently. Discuss each rule, allowing volunteers to share example sentences of each rule. Have the volunteers write their shared examples on the classroom board.

3. Distribute copies of the "Punctuate It and Rewrite It!" handout and the red or purple pens or pencils. Tell the students that to complete this handout, they will use their grading pen or pencil to write the correct punctuation in the incorrect sentence, and then they will rewrite the sentence correctly.

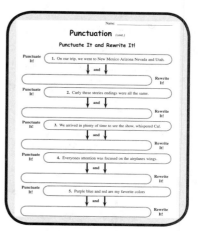

4. Display the "Punctuate It and Rewrite It!" handout transparency and read aloud the first sentence while the students read it silently. Ask volunteers to share how they would correct this sentence. Discuss the corrections for accuracy and add the correct punctuation to the sentence on the transparency. Then rewrite the sentence in the box labeled "Rewrite It!" Have the students do the same on their copy of the handout. Continue this procedure with the remaining sentences on the first page of the handout.

5. Tell the students to independently complete the remaining two pages of the handout. Then, after the handouts are complete, ask volunteers to come to the overhead, correct the sentence by writing in the missing punctuation on the transparency, and then rewrite the sentence below the original.

Wrap-Up

• To conclude the lesson, have the students write a response on a sheet of notebook paper to the following prompt: *Write several short paragraphs showing the correct use of the four punctuation rules learned in this lesson.*

• Divide the classroom board into five workstations. Ask volunteers to go to a workstation and write one of their paragraphs on the board. After all the volunteers have written their paragraphs, read and discuss each of them to make sure each is correct. Review the punctuation rules from the "Some Rules of Punctuation" reference sheet as they are addressed in the paragraphs.

Punctuation *(cont.)*

It's All About Punctuation

1. Friday will be cold dark and rainy.

_____

_____

_____

2. Fisher make sure the door is closed tightly.

_____

_____

_____

3. "Be sure you know how to do it" Luna warned "or you might get hurt."

_____

_____

_____

4. Kelly replied, I don't want to do the dishes tonight.

_____

_____

_____

5. His fathers hat blew off during that last gust of wind.

_____

_____

_____

Punctuation (cont.)

Some Rules of Punctuation

Commas in Series

• Use commas in between words, phrases, or clauses in a series.

Examples: All the lions, tigers, bears, and gorillas were asleep.

After school we walked to the park, fed the ducks, and played on the playground.

Commas in Direct Address

• Use commas to separate the person being spoken to from the rest of the sentence.

Examples: Selena, will you please go to the store for me?

I think you are right, Dad!

Commas and Quotation Marks in Dialogue

• Use commas to set off the exact words spoken by a person from the rest of a sentence.

• Use before and after spoken words of a person.

Examples: Barry said, "I believe you are correct."

"Yes," agreed Stacy, "I think you should go to the party."

Apostrophes in Possessives

• Use an apostrophe and s to make a singular noun possessive.

Example: My sister's cat is black.

• Use an apostrophe to make a plural noun ending in s possessive

Example: The giraffes' cages were being cleaned.

• Use an apostrophe and s to make a plural noun not ending in s possessive

Example: The children's book was new.

Name: _____

Punctuation *(cont.)*

Punctuate It and Rewrite It!

Punctuate It!

1. On our trip, we went to New Mexico Arizona Nevada and Utah.

↓ **and** ↓

Rewrite It!

Punctuate It!

2. Carly these stories endings were all the same.

↓ **and** ↓

Rewrite It!

Punctuate It!

3. We arrived in plenty of time to see the show, whispered Cal.

↓ **and** ↓

Rewrite It!

Punctuate It!

4. Everyones attention was focused on the airplanes wings.

↓ **and** ↓

Rewrite It!

Punctuate It!

5. Purple blue and red are my favorite colors

↓ **and** ↓

Rewrite It!

Punctuation (cont.)

Punctuate It and Rewrite It! (cont.)

Punctuate It!

6. We will be going home first Dennis.

and

Rewrite It!

Punctuate It!

7. She picked up her book threw it on the table and stormed out.

and

Rewrite It!

Punctuate It!

8. Mr. and Mrs. Collins here is the phone number you asked for

and

Rewrite It!

Punctuate It!

9. "We will start building it" said Kelly "but we will not finish it today."

and

Rewrite It!

Punctuate It!

10. The captain shouted All hands on deck!

and

Rewrite It!

Name: _____

Punctuation (cont.)

Punctuate It and Rewrite It! (cont.)

Punctuate It!

11. The salesmens meeting was supposed to be tomorrow.

and

Rewrite It!

Punctuate It!

12. I will be your best friend replied Samara even after you move.

and

Rewrite It!

Punctuate It!

13. The waitress found the babys bottle underneath the table.

and

Rewrite It!

Punctuate It!

14. Thank you Dionne for taking care of our cat, Snickers.

and

Rewrite It!

Punctuate It!

15. At the farm, Keith saw a horse an ox and a mule pulling a cart.

and

Rewrite It!

Organizing Ideas

Skill 23: The student will use planning strategies to generate topics and organize ideas (e.g., brainstorming, mapping, webbing).

Instructional Preparation

Materials:
- butcher paper (*one sheet per three-person group*)
- markers (*one set per three-person group*)

Duplicate the following (one per student, unless otherwise indicated):
- "Getting Ideas" handout

Prepare a transparency of the following:
- "Getting Ideas" handout

Recall

Before beginning the **Review** component, start a discussion with the following questions:
- ✳ What are some strategies a writer can use to decide on a topic to write about? (*brainstorming; looking through reference books*)
- ✳ What are some strategies a writer can use to organize different items in a paper? (*make a web; map the items; make an outline*)

Tell the class that sometimes it seems harder to come up with ideas to write about than it is to actually do the writing. Explain that today they will be using strategies to generate topics and organize their thoughts to help them with the writing process.

Review

1. Distribute the "Getting Ideas" handout and display the transparency. Tell the students they are going to review some strategies to help them decide on an idea and organize the supporting details for an informative paper on a pet. Ask the students what different kinds of pets they could write about. Write the suggestions in the "Brainstorming" section of the transparency. Decide as a class which kind of pet will be the topic of the paper.

2. Write the topic in the center of the "Webbing" section of the transparency and circle it. Have the students do the same on their copies. Explain that now they need to think about different things they would like to write about the topic. Ask the following question:

   ✳ What kinds of things can you write about (topic)? (*what they eat; where they live; their sleeping habits; what they look like; different varieties; how long they live*)

   As different ideas are shared, write them on the transparency as shown below.

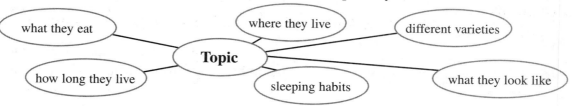

Point out to the students that they have the topic and different items to include in the paper. The next step is to organize the items so that they are in the order in which the students will write about them.

Organizing Ideas *(cont.)*

Review *(cont.)*

3. Direct the students' attention to the "Mapping" section of the handout. Explain to the students that there are many ways to organize a paper. They should think about what would be the best order for the paper. Explain to the class that a good way to organize a paper is to start with the broadest subject—a general idea. Tell the class that starting with "what they look like" would be a good beginning to the paper, since it gives the reader an overview of the pet. Write this down in the first box. Ask the following questions:

   ✳ What do you think should come next? Why? (*"where they live," because we have just described what they look like, and "where they live" is still a broad subject. It should come before their sleeping habits and what they eat*)

   Continue this line of questioning as you fill in the rest of the boxes, making sure each student justifies his or her response. Remind the students that the order can vary, as long as the paper makes sense and flows.

4. Place the students in groups of three. Distribute butcher paper and markers to each group. Tell the students that they will be using these three strategies to decide on a famous person and to organize the information that could be written about the person. Have the students brainstorm, create a web, and create a map on the butcher paper, using the handout as a guide. Circulate throughout the room to monitor student progress. Then have the members of each group display their work and discuss each of their steps.

5. Review the main points of the lesson by asking the following questions and discussing the responses:

   ✳ What is brainstorming? (*coming up with different ideas to write about*)

   ✳ How is a web used to organize ideas? (*You place the main idea in the center of the web, and the different things you can write about the main idea go all around it.*)

   ✳ How is a map used to organize ideas? (*It lets you place the items you are writing about in the order you are going to write about them.*)

Wrap-Up

   • To conclude this lesson, have the students use the reverse side of their handout to respond to the following prompts: *How can brainstorming help a writer decide on a topic? How can creating a web help a writer? How can creating a map help a writer?*

   • Ask several volunteers to share their answers. Use the responses to review brainstorming, webbing, and mapping as means of planning and organizing before writing.

Organizing Ideas *(cont.)*

Getting Ideas

Brainstorming

Webbing

Mapping

Verbs

Skill 24: The student will use regular, irregular, singular, plural, and helping verbs.

Instructional Preparation

Duplicate the following (one per student, unless otherwise indicated):

- "Verb Verbiage" reference sheet
- "Verb Voyage" handout
- "Superb Verbs" handout

Prepare a transparency of the following:

- "Verb Verbiage" reference sheet
- "Verb Voyage" handout
- "Superb Verbs" handout

Recall

Before beginning the **Review** component, facilitate a discussion based on the following questions:

❋ What are verbs? (*action words; doing words*)

❋ When are verbs used? (*when writing about what the subject of a sentence is doing*)

❋ What are some different kinds of verbs? (*regular, irregular, singular, plural, helping*)

Tell the students that in today's review lesson they will be using regular, irregular, singular, plural, and helping verbs.

Review

1. Distribute copies of the "Verb Verbiage" reference sheet and display the transparency. Explain that the circles on the web are all connected to the boxed word "Verbs" because they are all different categories of verbs. Read the parts of the web aloud and go over the examples. As each category and the examples are read, ask several volunteers to give other examples of verbs in that category, excluding the helping verbs category. Explain that some verbs fit into more than one category (for example, *were* is a helping verb, but it also is a plural verb).

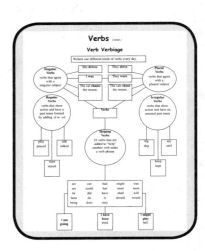

Verbs *(cont.)*

Review *(cont.)*

2. Distribute copies of the "Verb Voyage" handout and display the transparency. Explain that some incorrect verbs were used in the paragraph. Read the paragraph aloud while the students read along silently. Then ask the following question:

✳ Which verb is incorrect in the first sentence? *(was)*

Circle this on the transparency as students circle it on their handout. Then ask the following question:

✳ What verb should be used instead of *was*? *(were)*

Fill in this word in the blank in the bottom paragraph as the students fill it in on their handout. Continue this process with the rest of the handout.

3. Have the students pair up. Distribute copies of the "Superb Verbs" handout. Have the students complete the handout according to the directions. Explain to them that each student is responsible for completing his or her own copy of the handout.

4. Display the "Superb Verbs" transparency. Ask volunteers to write responses on the transparency. Have each volunteer explain his or her response and discuss the responses for accuracy.

Wrap-Up

• To conclude this lesson, have the students use the reverse side of their "Superb Verbs" handout to respond to the following: *List the five types of verbs covered in this lesson and explain how they are used. Then give an example of each type of verb.*

• Ask volunteers to share their responses. Discuss the responses and use them to review how to use the five types of verbs in sentences.

Verbs *(cont.)*

Verb Verbiage

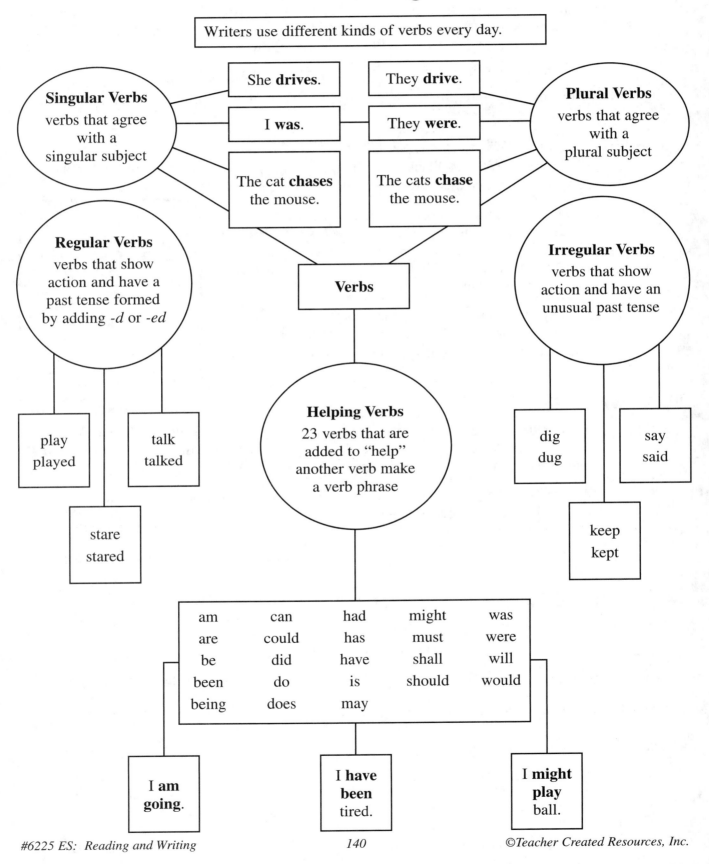

Writers use different kinds of verbs every day.

Singular Verbs
verbs that agree with a singular subject

Plural Verbs
verbs that agree with a plural subject

She **drives**.

They **drive**.

I **was**.

They **were**.

The cat **chases** the mouse.

The cats **chase** the mouse.

Verbs

Regular Verbs
verbs that show action and have a past tense formed by adding *-d* or *-ed*

Irregular Verbs
verbs that show action and have an unusual past tense

play
played

talk
talked

stare
stared

dig
dug

say
said

keep
kept

Helping Verbs
23 verbs that are added to "help" another verb make a verb phrase

am	can	had	might	was
are	could	has	must	were
be	did	have	shall	will
been	do	is	should	would
being	does	may		

I am going.

I have been tired.

I might play ball.

Name: _____

Verbs *(cont.)*

Verb Voyage

The notorious pirates was sailing on the ocean. The nervous captain see them through his trusted telescope. "We is going to had to wage war!" say the captain loudly. The crew replied angrily, "We know that the pirates would spoils our day!" The captain tell his sailors to get the cannons ready for a battle. They had the cannonballs stacked and prepared to blast when the captain shout, "Wait! These pirates is from Pittsburgh! Grabs the bats!"

The notorious pirates _____ sailing on the ocean. The nervous captain _____ them through his trusted telescope. "We _____ going to _____ to wage war!" _____ the captain loudly. The crew replied angrily, "We _____ that the pirates would _____ our day!" The captain _____ his sailors to get the cannons ready for a battle. They had the cannonballs stacked and prepared to blast when the captain _____ , "Wait! These pirates _____ from Pittsburgh! _____ the bats!"

Verbs *(cont.)*

Superb Verbs

Directions: Read the paragraph on the ticket. Circle all the verbs that need to be changed. Use correct verbs to fill in the blanks in the bottom paragraph.

Concert

	City Stadium	
	Sections: 45	
	Row: 12	
	Seat: 4	
	Date: Next week	

The girls was excited. Tonight they were going to saw their favorite singing group, the Electric Hip Hops. "I just loves the way T.K. sing 'You Be the Only Girl I Will Probably Forgot,'" said Tracy.

"Shamika like it when Bobby sing 'I Were Crazy,' say Maria. The parking lot were empty when they arrived at the stadium. Tracy look at the tickets. "Oh no!" she said. "These tickets is for next week!"

The girls _____ excited. Tonight they were going to _____ their favorite singing group, the Electric Hip Hops. "I just _____ the way T.K. _____ 'You _____ the Only Girl I Will Probably _____ ,'" said Tracy.

"Shamika _____ it when Bobby _____ 'I _____ Crazy,'" _____ Maria.

The parking lot _____ empty when they arrived at the stadium. Tracy _____ at the tickets. "Oh no!" she said. "These tickets _____ for next week!"

Simple and Compound Sentences

Skill 25: The student will use simple and compound sentences.

Instructional Preparation

Materials:

- one yellow and one pink highlighter (*one set per student pair*)

Duplicate the following (one per student, unless otherwise indicated):

- "From Simple to Compound" reference sheet
- "Simple Compound Practice" handout

Prepare a transparency of the following:

- "From Simple to Compound" reference sheet
- "Simple Compound Practice" handout

Recall

Before beginning the **Review** component, facilitate a discussion based on the following questions:

- ✳ What is a simple sentence? (*an independent clause that contains a subject and a verb*)
- ✳ What is a compound sentence? (*two simple sentences joined together by a comma and a conjunction, such as "for," "and," "nor," "but," "or," "yet," or "so"*)

Explain to the students that in today's review they will be using simple and compound sentences.

Review

1. Distribute copies of the "From Simple to Compound" reference sheet and display the first page of the transparency. Read the information in the top box aloud while the students read it silently. Ask a volunteer to read the first example. Underline "John" and explain that it is the subject of the sentence because it is whom or what the sentence is about. Underline "went," using a different color and explain that it is the verb because it describes what the subject is doing. Continue this procedure with the three other examples. Model writing simple sentences in the form of the examples in the "Simple Sentence Practice" section. Have the students do the same on their copy of the reference sheet.

2. Direct the students' attention to the second page of the reference sheet and display the transparency. Read the sentence in the top box aloud while the students read it silently. Ask a volunteer to read the sentence and the examples in the "Conjunctions" box. Emphasize that conjunctions are the words used to link two simple sentences to create a compound sentence.

Simple and Compound Sentences *(cont.)*

Review *(cont.)*

3. Direct attention to the "Compound Sentence Examples" section. Read the first sentence as the students read it silently. Underline the first and second simple sentences in the first sentence. Point out that these are simple sentences. Underline the comma and the word "but" with a different color. Explain that the two simple sentences have been joined by the comma and the conjunction "but" to create a compound sentence. Ask volunteers to underline the simple sentences, the comma, and the conjunction in the other two examples on the transparency. Model writing compound sentences in the "Compound Sentence Practice" section. Have the students do the same on their copy of the reference sheet.

4. Have the students pair up. Distribute copies of the "Simple Compound Practice" handout and the highlighters. Tell the students to follow the directions to complete the handout. Explain that they may refer to the "From Simple to Compound" reference sheet while working and that each student is responsible for completing his or her own handout.

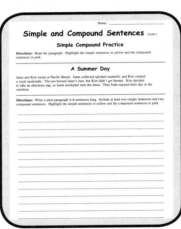

5. Display the "Simple Compound Practice" transparency. Ask volunteers to write one sentence from their paragraphs on the transparency. Discuss each response for accuracy.

Wrap-Up

- To conclude this lesson, have the students use the reverse side of their "Simple Compound Practice" handout to respond to the following prompts: *Write an example of a simple and a compound sentence. Explain how simple and compound sentences are different.*

- Ask volunteers to share their responses. Discuss the responses, and use them to review how to use simple and compound sentences.

Simple and Compound Sentences *(cont.)*

From Simple to Compound

A *simple sentence* is also called an *independent clause*. It has a subject and a verb.

Simple Sentence Examples

Some have one subject and one verb.

Example: John went to the game.

Some have more than one subject and one verb.

Example: John and Ken went to the game.

Some have one subject and more than one verb.

Example: John went to the game and cheered the team.

Some have more than one subject and more than one verb.

Example: John and Ken went to the game and cheered the team.

Simple Sentence Practice

1. _____ _____ .
           (subject)   *(verb)*

2. _____ and _____ .
           (subject)   *(subject)*

   _____ .
           (verb)

3. _____ and _____ .
           (subject)   *(subject)*

   _____ .
           (verb)

Simple and Compound Sentences *(cont.)*

From Simple to Compound *(cont.)*

A *compound sentence* is a sentence made up of two simple sentences joined by a comma and a *conjunction*.

Conjunctions

Conjunctions are words that help connect two simple sentences

for   and   nor   but   or   yet   so

Compound Sentence Examples

1. I colored the giraffe, *but* Tamara colored the leopard.
2. Todd picked the red bookmark, *so* Rosa stacked the books.
3. Kari bought the slacks, *and* Juanita bought the blouse.

Compound Sentence Practice

1. _____   _____
   (simple sentence)   *(conjunction)*

   _____ .
   (simple sentence)

2. _____   _____
   (simple sentence)   *(conjunction)*

   _____ .
   (simple sentence)

3. _____   _____
   (simple sentence)   *(conjunction)*

   _____ .
   (simple sentence)

Simple and Compound Sentences *(cont.)*

Simple Compound Practice

Directions: Read the paragraph. Highlight the simple sentences in yellow and the compound sentences in pink.

A Summer Day

Janet and Kim swam at Pacific Beach. Janet collected spiraled seashells, and Kim created a royal sandcastle. The sun burned Janet's face, but Kim didn't get burned. Kim decided to take an afternoon nap, so Janet snorkeled near the shore. They both enjoyed their day in the sunshine.

Directions: Write a short paragraph 4–6 sentences long. Include at least two simple sentences and two compound sentences. Highlight the simple sentences in yellow and the compound sentences in pink.

_____

_____

_____

_____

_____

_____

_____

_____

_____

_____

_____

_____

Nouns and Pronouns

Skill 26: The student will use singular nouns, plural nouns, and pronouns.

Instructional Preparation

Duplicate the following (one per student, unless otherwise indicated):

- "Nouns and Pronouns" reference sheet
- "Change Is Good!" handout

Prepare a transparency of the following:

- "Nouns and Pronouns" reference sheet
- "Practice Makes Perfect" sheet
- "Change Is Good!" handout

Recall

Before beginning the **Review** component, facilitate a discussion based on the following questions:

- ✳ What is a noun? (*a person, place, thing, or idea*)

- ✳ What kinds of nouns are there? (*common nouns, proper nouns, singular nouns, plural nouns*)

- ✳ What is a singular noun? (*a noun that names one person, place, thing, or idea*)

- ✳ What is a plural noun? (*a noun that names two or more people, places, things, or ideas*)

- ✳ Why is it important to know when to use a singular or plural noun? (*It allows a writer to convey his or her ideas better; it allows the reader to better understand what he or she is reading.*)

- ✳ What is a pronoun? (*a word that can be used in place of a noun*)

- ✳ Why is it important to know when to use pronouns? (*Since pronouns replace a noun, a writer needs to know which pronoun to use when referring to people, places, object, and ideas.*)

Explain that in the review lesson the students will be using singular nouns, plural nouns, and pronouns in the context of a sentence.

Review

1. Distribute the first page of the "Nouns and Pronouns" reference sheet and display the transparency. Ask a volunteer to read the information in the "Singular Nouns" section while the rest of the students read it silently. Discuss what singular nouns are and ask volunteers to share singular nouns. Write the singular nouns on the board underneath headings specifying "Person," "Place," "Thing," and "Idea."

Nouns and Pronouns *(cont.)*

Review *(cont.)*

2. Ask several volunteers to read the rules in the "Plural Nouns" section of the handout while the rest of the students read them silently. Discuss the different rules pertaining to making plural nouns. Ask volunteers to assist you in writing the plurals of all the nouns written on the board during step 1. Make sure each of the rules for making plural nouns is covered using these words. If all the rules for making plural nouns have not been covered, add nouns that cover these rules.

3. Display the top section of the "Practice Makes Perfect" transparency. Explain that in each sentence the noun needs to be changed either from plural to singular or from singular to plural. Read the first sentence under the heading "Using Singular and Plural Nouns" while the students read along silently. Explain that the word "reservation" needs to be plural. Ask the following question:

   ✳ Which rule should be followed to make this word plural? (*Add "s" to the end of the word.*)

   Discuss the responses and write the word "reservations" on the line next to the first sentence on the transparency. Then, ask a volunteer to read sentence 2 under the heading "Using Singular and Plural Nouns" while the rest of the students read along silently. Ask the following questions:

   ✳ Which word in the sentence needs to be changed? (*boss*)

   ✳ What needs to be done to the word "boss"? (*It needs to be made plural.*)

   ✳ Which rule should be used to make this word plural? (*If a noun ends in "s," add "es."*)

   Discuss the responses, and write the word "bosses" on the line next to the second sentence on the transparency. Continue the procedure described in this step for the remaining sentences in the "Using Singular and Plural Nouns" section.

4. Distribute the second page of the "Nouns and Pronouns" reference sheet and display the transparency. Ask a volunteer to read the information in the "Pronoun" section while the rest of the students read along silently. Discuss the differences in each sentence, explaining that pronouns can be used in different ways. Read and discuss the remaining sections on the reference sheet, and ask for volunteers to share a sentence using some of the different pronouns listed. Write appropriate sentences on the classroom board.

Nouns and Pronouns *(cont.)*

Review *(cont.)*

5. Display the "Using Pronouns" section of the "Practice Makes Perfect" transparency. Read the first sentence under the "Using Pronouns" section while the rest of the students read it silently. Ask the following questions:

   ✳ Which nouns in this sentence can be replaced with pronouns? (*Amelia, temperature*)

   ✳ What new sentence can be made by replacing these nouns with pronouns? (*She said it was 54 degrees outside.*)

   ✳ What kind of pronoun is "she" in this sentence? (*subject pronoun*)

   ✳ What kind of pronoun is "it" in this sentence? (*object pronoun*)

   ✳ Did using pronouns instead of nouns improve the sentence? Why or why not? (*No, it did not improve the sentence much. But if this sentence was in a paragraph, it might be good to replace her name with a pronoun; it would also be good to say this sentence using pronouns if you were discussing the outside temperature with someone and it did not matter who told you the temperature.*)

   Discuss the responses for accuracy, circling "Amelia" and "temperature" on the transparency; rewrite the sentence on the line using the pronouns. Continue the procedure described in this step for sentences 2 through 4 in the "Using Pronouns" section. Then, read number 5 aloud while the students read along silently. Ask the following question:

   ✳ Which pronoun is missing from this sentence? (*her*)

   Discuss the responses. Tell the students that "her" is the correct pronoun, since this sentence is referring to the girl in the first sentence of number 5.

6. Have the students get into pairs. Distribute copies of the "Change Is Good!" handout. Read aloud each set of directions while the students read them silently. Have each pair complete the handout together, with each student being responsible for completing his or her own handout. When the pairs have finished their handout, display the "Change Is Good!" transparency. Ask volunteers to share their answers. Discuss the answers for accuracy, and ask volunteers to write appropriate answers on the transparency.

Wrap-Up

• To conclude the lesson, have the students use the reverse side of their "Change Is Good!" handouts to write responses to the following prompts: *Write what singular and plural nouns are, and write a sentence showing an example of each. Circle the singular nouns and underline the plural nouns in each sentence. Write what a pronoun is, and write a short paragraph using several examples of pronouns. Circle each pronoun.*

• Ask several volunteers to share their responses. Use the responses to review how to use plural nouns, singular nouns, and pronouns in the context of a sentence.

Nouns and Pronouns *(cont.)*

Nouns and Pronouns

Singular Nouns

A noun is *singular* when it means only one person, place, thing, or idea. The following are singular nouns: *panther, castle, scholar.*

Plural Nouns

A noun is *plural* when it means more than one person, place, thing, or idea. The following are plural nouns: *panthers, castles, scholars.*

A plural noun is made by adding *s* to the end of the word.

report ⟶ reports

When a word ends in *ch, sh, s, x,* or *z,* you need to add *es* to the end of the word.

crouch ⟶ crouches
vanish ⟶ vanishes
moss ⟶ mosses
index ⟶ indexes
buzz ⟶ buzzes

Most nouns that end in *f* or *fe,* such as *calf* and *wife,* are made plural by changing the *f* or *fe* to *v* and adding *es* to the end of the word.

calf ⟶ calves
wife ⟶ wives

Some exceptions are as follows: *chief, roof,* and *safe.*
Just add *s* to the end of these words.

If a noun ends in a vowel and *y,* just add *s* to the end of the word.

volley ⟶ volleys

If a noun ends in a consonant and *y,* change the *y* to an *i* and add *es* to the end of the word.

fly ⟶ flies
story ⟶ stories
city ⟶ cities

If a noun ends in a vowel and *o,* just add *s* to the end of the word.

zoo ⟶ zoos

If a noun ends in a consonant and *o,* add *es* to the end of the word.

volcano ⟶ volcanoes

Some exceptions are as follows: *solo* and *piano.*
Just add *s* to the end of these words.

Nouns and Pronouns *(cont.)*

Pronouns

A *pronoun* is a word you use in place of a noun.

This sentence is correct:

- *Amy* saw *Amy's* mother folding *Amy's* clothes.

However, using pronouns can improve the sentence:

- *Amy* say *her* mother folding *her* clothes.

You can also replace a name using a pronoun:

- *She* saw *her* mother folding *her* clothes.

Subject pronouns

These pronouns replace the name of the subject.

- *John* was in the kitchen when *Paula* called.
- *He* was in the kitchen when *she* called.

Some subject pronouns include *I, you, he, she, it, we, you, they.*

Object pronouns

These pronouns replace the object in a sentence:

- Gina said *the earthquake* was 5.2 on the Richter scale.
- Gina said *it* was 5.2 on the Richter scale.

These pronouns can also replace the object of the verb or preposition:

- Harry gave the book to his mom.
- Harry gave the book to her.

Some object pronouns include *me, you, him, her, it, us, you, them.*

Possessive pronouns

These pronouns replace a noun or phrase that shows ownership:

- The DVD belongs to George and Martha.
- That is their DVD
- That DVD belongs to them.

Some possessive pronouns are *my, your, his, her, its, our, their, mine, yours, hers, ours, theirs.*

Nouns and Pronouns *(cont.)*

Practice Makes Perfect

Using Singular and Plural Nouns

_____ **1.** We need to make reservation for dinner.

_____ **2.** All the boss were in a meeting until 4:00.

_____ **3.** There was only one dominoes facedown on the board.

_____ **4.** The lumberjack was sharpening his three ax for the following day.

_____ **5.** The scouts need to have a new mottoes by the end of the meeting.

_____ **6.** Tunnier Builders is currently making plans to build four new community in our area.

_____ **7.** Marge saw a horses running in the field.

Using Pronouns

1. Amelia said the temperature was 54 degrees outside.

_____

2. Denise will demonstrate the way Tim and Paula need to wrap the presents.

_____

3. The refreshments were brought by Jan, Pete, Alice, and me.

_____

4. Sarah and Sarah's friend went to the amusement park with Sarah's family and Sarah's friend's family.

_____

5. "Wanda just handed in her book report. It's just like _____ to be finished first!" said Tyler.

Nouns and Pronouns (cont.)

Change Is Good!

Directions: Read each sentence below. Write the correct form of the noun on the line provided.

_____ 1. Tony couldn't decide between the two sombrero.

_____ 2. Jeff has been accepted at three university next year.

_____ 3. The starting salaries for the manager position is $40,000 a year.

_____ 4. Mr. Reed won first prize for the single largest squashes at the state fair.

_____ 5. The Eskimos' igloo are dome-shaped and made of snow and ice.

_____ 6. You will have sixes additional problems for homework tonight.

_____ 7. The chief were worried about the tribal meeting.

_____ 8. "A zeroes will be given for each overdue assignment," she said.

_____ 9. "Do not walk in that trenches; you'll catch a cold," said the mother.

_____ 10. Mom embroidered two of my handkerchief with my initials.

_____ 11. We have one cream-colored vanities still in stock.

_____ 12. All the new business in the office building will open next Monday.

_____ 13. The maintenance men make sure they check each of the pulley before leaving for the day.

_____ 14. Dad sharpened all the kitchen knife with his new sharpener.

_____ 15. The department store has a sale: for every mattresses you buy, you receive a free pillow.

Nouns and Pronouns (cont.)

Change Is Good (cont.)

Directions: Rewrite each sentence using correct pronouns.

1. Mary had promised to return Marty's book.

   _____

2. Next Wednesday, Abe, Ben, and I are going to see Jack and Jeff play baseball.

   _____

3. Nancy bought Nancy's sweater last Thursday.

   _____

4. Carl saw the volcano erupt on a vacation with Carl's parents, Betty and Fred.

   _____

5. The play that I saw with Mark and Molly was wonderful.

   _____

Directions: Fill in the blank with the correct pronoun: *me, my, mine, our, ours.*

6. She was talking on the phone to _____.

7. _____ is the first scout troop to win the award.

8. I can't find _____ essay anywhere!

9. "Excuse me, but could you throw us _____ ball?" yelled Ben.

10. "It's not yours, it's _____!" screamed Jan's baby brother.

Informative Writing

Skill 27: The student will write to inform (e.g., to explain, to describe, to report, to narrate).

Instructional Preparation

Choose or prepare a transparency of the following:
- a painting by a famous artist

Duplicate the following (one per student, unless otherwise indicated):
- "Writing to Inform" reference sheet
- "Planning to Write to Inform" handout
- "Expository and Narrative Paragraphs" passage

Prepare a transparency of the following:
- "Writing to Inform" reference sheet
- "Planning to Write to Inform" handout
- "Expository and Narrative Paragraphs" passage

Recall

Before beginning the **Review** component, start a discussion based on the following questions:

❋ What does it mean when you are writing a paragraph to inform? (*You are giving information; you are explaining how to do something; you are describing something to tell someone about it; you are telling a story of a true event.*)

❋ What is a descriptive paragraph? (*a paragraph that gives a detailed account of a person, place, thing, or event*)

❋ What is an expository paragraph? (*a paragraph that explains a subject; a paragraph that gives directions; a paragraph that shows how to do something*)

❋ What is a narrative paragraph? (*a paragraph that tells a true story about a memorable event or an important experience in your life*)

Let the students know that they will be writing descriptive, expository, and narrative paragraphs.

Review

1. Distribute copies of the "Writing to Inform" reference sheet and display the transparency. Ask volunteers to read each section of the reference sheet aloud while the rest of the students read it silently. Discuss each type of informative paragraph.

2. Distribute copies of "Expository and Narrative Paragraphs" and display the transparency. Read aloud the expository passage while the students read it silently. Discuss what the passage is mostly about. Then ask the following question:

   ❋ What makes this an expository paragraph? (*It gives information that explains about an object; it uses definitions and details to describe the object.*)

   Discuss the responses. Lead a discussion about the elements of expository paragraphs.

3. Distribute copies of the "Expository and Narrative Paragraphs" passage and display the transparency. Read aloud the narrative passage while the students read it silently. Discuss what the passage is mostly about. Then ask the following question:

   ❋ What makes this a narrative paragraph? (*It tells the story of an actual event; it has details that explain the 5 Ws (who, what, when, where, and why,); it uses chronological time to tell the story; it uses specific details to tell the story.*)

   Discuss the responses. Lead a discussion about the elements of narrative paragraphs.

Review *(cont.)*

4. Tell the students that the class is going to write a descriptive paragraph together based on observations made while looking at a famous painting. Display the chosen painting so that it is clearly visible to all the students. Tell the students the name of the painting and the artist who painted it. Allow the students time to examine the painting.

5. Display the "Planning to Write to Inform" transparency. Complete the sentence at the top of the page by writing the word "descriptive" on the first blank line and the title of the painting on the second blank line. Then ask the following questions:

   ✳ What will be the topic of this descriptive paragraph? (*Accept reasonable responses.*)

   ✳ What would be an appropriate main-idea statement that would best show what this paragraph would mainly be about? (*Accept reasonable responses.*)

   Discuss the appropriate responses and write them in the boxes labeled "Topic" and "Main Idea" on the transparency. Then continue the discussion, asking volunteers to share their observations and descriptions of the painting. Write their observations and descriptions in the ovals connected to the arrows from the "Main Idea" box.

6. Once an ample number of observations and descriptions have been shared, write, with the students' assistance, a descriptive paragraph about the painting on a sheet of chart paper. When the descriptive paragraph is finished, discuss it to make sure it contains all the components or elements of an effective descriptive paragraph.

7. Tell the students that they are going to write their own paragraphs. Distribute copies of "Planning to Write to Inform." Have one-third of the class write a descriptive paragraph, one-third write an expository paragraph, and one-third write a narrative paragraph. Tell them to use their handout to plan their paragraph, and then write it on a sheet of notebook paper.

8. After the students have written their paragraph, have them get into three groups: the descriptive group, the expository group, and the narrative group. Allow volunteers in each group to read their paragraph to the group. Tell the groups to discuss each paragraph that is read to make sure it contains all the components or elements of an effective informative paragraph.

9. In a whole-group setting, ask volunteers to share their paragraph. Have the students determine the type of paragraph and discuss each shared paragraph to make sure it contains all the components or elements of an effective informative paragraph.

Wrap-Up

- To conclude the lesson, ask the following questions: *What are the components or elements that make an effective descriptive paragraph? What are the components or elements that make an effective expository paragraph? What are the components or elements that make an effective narrative paragraph?*

- Ask volunteers to share their responses. Use the responses to facilitate a review of how to write descriptive, expository, and narrative paragraphs.

Informative Writing *(cont.)*

Writing to Inform

Descriptive Paragraph

* ✳ a paragraph that provides a detailed description of a person, place, thing, or event

* ✳ uses descriptive words (e.g., adjectives, adverbs) and phrases

* ✳ uses sensory descriptions (e.g., hear, see, smell, taste, touch)

* ✳ needs specific details to accurately describe the person, place, thing, or event

Expository Paragraph

* ✳ a paragraph that gives information that explains a subject, gives directions, or shows how something is done

* ✳ requires complete understanding of the subject or topic

* ✳ uses effective details to explain about a specific subject

* ✳ uses step-by-step directions to show how a task is completed

* ✳ uses specific details to accurately explain how something is done or made

Narrative Paragraph

* ✳ a paragraph that tells a story about an actual event in your life that is memorable or important

* ✳ provides details that answer the 5 Ws (who, what, when, where, and why)

* ✳ uses time order to organize details

* ✳ needs specific details to accurately tell the story

Informative Writing *(cont.)*
Expository and Narrative Paragraphs

Expository

Zip It!

One of the simplest machines of modern time is the zipper. It is one of the most used machines in everyday life. You find zippers on pants, coats, dresses, suitcases, sleeping bags, and tents. The zipper uses two of the oldest and simplest tools: the wedge and the hook. The wedge is an object with a slanted surface. When a wedge is pushed against an object, it will push the object right or left. An example of this is a plow on a farm. When the plow is pushed, the dirt is sent to the left and right of the plow. The hook is a curved piece that is used to grab onto something else. The zipper track is made of dozens of teeth, or hooks. When a person pulls up on a zipper tab, all the hooks lock together. This is done with a slide, which is made of wedges. As the slide moves up, its inclined edges push the teeth together. For this to work, all the teeth must be the same size and shape, and they must also be lined up perfectly on the zipper track. When a person pulls down on a zipper tab, the wedge in the slide forces the teeth away from each other. This is how a zipper works.

Narrative

I Can Still Remember

I can still remember it just as if it were yesterday. I am about to go to middle school, which will be a whole new experience in itself. But I will always remember my first day of school—my first day of kindergarten. I was so excited to start school that I thought I would burst. I did not go to preschool; instead, I had a sitter who was a wonderful and loving lady named Nina. She taught me all kinds of things. She taught me how to cook, sew, and do crafts. She also started teaching me the letters of the alphabet and the sounds they made. But I was ready for school, and I was only four years old. On my first day of school, both of my parents dropped me off at school, because the first day of school seems to be a big day for parents, too. They stood right outside the playground gate while I hesitantly walked to the cone that marked my class's line. Once I got to the line, I stood there like a good little girl. After about 10 seconds of me waving to my parents and them waving back, I got a tap on my shoulder. I turned around, and a girl with pretty, long blond hair was standing in front of me. She said, "Hi, my name is Elise. Do you want to go to the playground and play with me?" Being the shy girl that I was, I immediately said "yes." Elise grabbed my hand, and we were off to the playground. This is memorable to me because ever since then, Elise and I have been inseparable. She is my best friend now and forever.

Name: _____

Informative Writing *(cont.)*

Planning to Write to Inform

I am writing a(an) _____ paragraph about _____

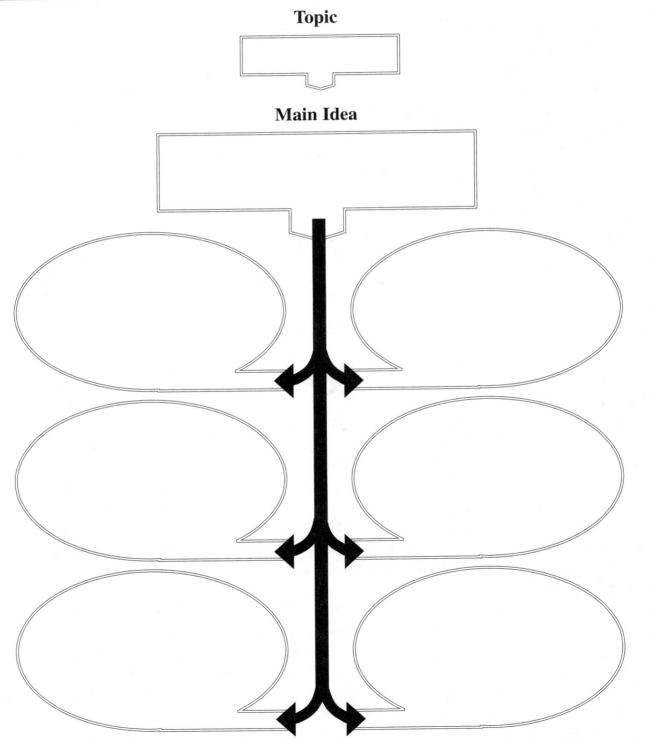

Topic

Main Idea

Persuasive Writing

Skill 28: The student will write to influence (e.g., to persuade, to argue, to request).

Instructional Preparation

Duplicate the following (one per student, unless otherwise indicated):
- "Writing to Influence" reference sheet
- "Influencing" reference sheet
- "I Can Influence You" handout

Prepare a transparency of the following:
- "Writing to Influence" reference sheet
- "Influencing" reference sheet
- "I Can Influence You" handout

Recall

Before beginning the **Review** component, facilitate a discussion based on the following questions:

❋ How can a writer try to influence a reader? (*by trying to persuade the reader; by arguing a point; by making a request*)

❋ What does it mean to persuade a reader? (*writing from a particular point of view so that the reader will see things the writer's way*)

❋ What does it mean to argue a point? (*arguing a case by explaining why one side is wrong and the other is right*)

❋ What does it mean to make a request? (*to ask for something*)

Explain to the students that in today's review they will be writing to influence the reader.

Review

1. Distribute the "Writing to Influence" reference sheet and display the transparency. Explain that sometimes a writer wants to influence the way the reader thinks. This page shows three different ways that a writer can influence the reader. Ask volunteers to read each section of the reference sheet. Discuss each type of writing and ask volunteers to share ideas for writing each type. Record the ideas on the transparency beneath each type of writing. Have the students do the same on their copy of the handout.

2. Distribute copies of the "Influencing" reference sheet and display the transparency. Show only the "Persuade" passage. Read the passage aloud as the students read along silently. Ask the following question:

   ❋ How do you know this is an example of a passage that persuades? (*The writer gives his or her point of view about why the historic homes should not be torn down.*) Discuss the responses.

3. Display only the "Argue" passage on the transparency. Read the passage aloud as the students read along silently. Ask the following question:

   ❋ How do you know this is an example of a passage that argues a point? (*The writer addresses both sides of an issue and explains why one side is right and the other is wrong.*) Discuss the responses.

Persuasive Writing *(cont.)*

Review *(cont.)*

4. Display only the "Request" passage. Read the passage aloud to the students as they read along silently. Ask the following question:

   ✳ How do you know this is an example of a passage that makes a request? (*The letter asks for a donation.*) Discuss the responses.

5. Display the "I Can Influence You" transparency. Tell the students that as a class they will be writing a persuasive paragraph. The topic will be "bedtime for fifth graders." The point of view will be that bedtime for all fifth graders should be 11:00 P.M. Record this information in the appropriate spaces on the transparency. Ask the following question:

   ✳ What reasons can the writer give to help persuade the reader that bedtime for all fifth graders should be 11:00 P.M.? (*Responses will vary; accept all reasonable responses.*)

   Record the students' responses on the transparency in the "Support" section of the handout.

6. Once an adequate number of support responses have been shared, write in the box, with the students' help, a persuasive paragraph about why fifth graders should have a bedtime of 11:00 P.M. Use the information in the "Support" section of the handout. Read and discuss the paragraph when it is finished. Be sure it contains the necessary elements of a persuasive paragraph.

7. Tell the students that they are going to write their own paragraph to influence. Distribute copies of the "I Can Influence You" handout. Divide the class into three groups. Tell one group that they will be writing a passage to persuade, the second that they will be writing a passage to argue a point, and the third that they will be writing a passage to make a request. Encourage the students to use their "Writing to Influence" and "Influencing" reference sheets as guides. Go around the room to monitor the students' progress and give advice. When the students are finished, ask several volunteers to share their paragraph. Ask the class these questions:

   ✳ How did the writer persuade/argue a point/make a request? (*Answers will vary.*)

   ✳ Should the writer have added anything to make his or her point clearer? (*Answers will vary.*)

   Discuss the answers.

Wrap-Up

- To conclude this lesson, have the students use the reverse side of their "Writing to Influence" reference sheet to respond to the following questions: *How can a writer persuade? How can a writer argue a point? How can a writer make a request?*

- Allow volunteers to share their responses. Discuss the responses and use them to review the differences between influencing a reader by persuading, arguing, and making a request.

Persuasive Writing *(cont.)*

Writing to Influence

Persuade

writing to have someone understand something from a certain point of view; writing in a way that leads the reader to have a certain opinion

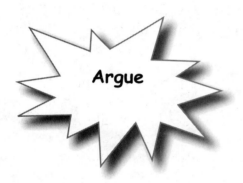

Argue

writing to state a case by explaining why one side is right and one is wrong

Request

writing to ask for something or to ask someone to do something

Persuasive Writing *(cont.)*

Influencing

Persuade

Do not let the city tear down the historic homes in the lakeside area. Most of these homes are well over 100 years old. They are a part of our town's history. In addition, most of these homes have been owned by the same families since they were built. For these families, losing their homes means losing their heritage. Finally, these homes have a distinct architecture. Tearing them down would be like destroying art. Join me in opposing this measure at the next city council meeting. Do not let the city destroy something that makes our town unique.

Argue

Most agree that the referee at last night's basketball game made a mistake. He did not count the basket made in the last seconds of the game. Parents, players, and fans all agree that the ball was in the air when the final buzzer went off. They want the referee's decision overturned.

However, the referee does not agree. He says that the ball was not in the air when the final buzzer went off. He states that the ball was still in the player's hands, which prompted him to not count the last basket. He wants his decision to stand.

Clearly, the referee is right in his decision. The referee has the best view of what goes on in the game because he is on the court. Also, it is the referee's job to watch the ball. He knows best what to look for. In addition, the basketball rulebook states that the referee's call is final. Even though the parents, players, and fans are upset, the referee's decision should stand.

Request

Dear Citizen,

Donations are desperately needed for the local food bank. One out of every three families in our community is living without an adequate food supply. The food bank needs to collect 4,000 cans of food this month. Every can will help. Please take the time to visit one of the collection sites and donate canned food. Thank you in advance for your generosity.

Flynn Nolan

President of Feed the People

Persuasive Writing *(cont.)*

I Can Influence You

Type of Paragraph: _____

Topic: _____

Point(s) of View: _____

_____

Support: _____

_____

_____

_____

_____

_____

PAL Packets

Introduction

PAL Packets are an important component of the *Essential Skills* series. PAL stands for "Parent Assisted Learning," and each PAL Packet lesson is meant to supplement student learning with a short activity that gives parents and guardians the tools to help their children practice important skills.

The lessons listed below can be found in both English and Spanish on the CDs that accompany this book. A sample PAL lesson has been provided in the pages that follow.

. . . .

Author's Purpose ✳ *Learn how an author uses specific details to bring out his or her point in writing.*

Compare and Contrast Characters ✳ *Learn how an author uses similarities and differences in a story to show the characters' individual qualities.*

Fact and Opinion ✳ *Learn to identify statements of fact and statements of opinion in stories that are meant to persuade the reader.*

Homonyms ✳ *Learn to identify homonyms, words that are pronounced in the same way but have different meanings.*

Inference ✳ *Learn to make inferences—broad conclusions based on supporting evidence—about a character's reasons for action in a fictional story.*

List Sources ✳ *Learn to write a bibliography to list source materials for reports.*

Locate Information ✳ *Learn to use the different parts of a book to locate information.*

Plot ✳ *Learn how to understand the plot of a story to determine the importance of each action or event.*

Problem Resolution ✳ *Learn how to understand the conflicts (problems) and their solutions in a story.*

Respond to the Text ✳ *Learn how to write a response to a question about the main character in a nonfiction story.*

Sentence Patterns ✳ *Learn to identify the three main parts of a sentence: the subject, the predicate, and the modifiers.*

Summarize ✳ *Learn to sum up the main idea and supporting details of a nonfiction selection.*

Theme ✳ *Learn to find the theme, the major idea that a fictional story says about life.*

Parent Assisted Learning (PAL)

Reading/Language Arts
Grade 5
Fact and Opinion

Dear Parent or Guardian:

Your son or daughter is currently learning to identify statements of fact and statements of opinion in stories. Here is your chance to help him or her practice this important skill.

In this PAL Packet you will find a short activity for you and your son or daughter to do. Please do the activity and "The Back Page." Then sign your name on "The Back Page" and have your son or daughter return it by _____.

Thanks for your help.

Sincerely,

_____

Fact vs. Opinion

Parent Pointer

When authors write to persuade a reader, they present both facts and opinions for the reader to consider. By being able to identify a statement of opinion, a reader knows the way an author feels about a particular subject. An opinion is a conclusion or judgment held with confidence. A fact, on the other hand, is something that actually exists, something that has actually occurred, or something known by observation or experience to be true or real. By being able to identify facts, the reader can determine whether the author's opinion is something he or she can agree with.

Student Directions

With a parent or partner, read the story "Pure Genius" on the next page. As you read, think about the statements that the author is using. When you have finished reading, you should complete the "Fact vs. Opinion" worksheet by following the directions. Then discuss your answers with your parent or partner.

Talk About It

After you have finished the activity, turn to "The Back Page" to show what you know.

Now go have some fun with the activity!

Pure Genius

"First, be sure a thing is wanted or needed. Then, go ahead." These are the words of Thomas Alva Edison, the greatest inventor the world has ever known.

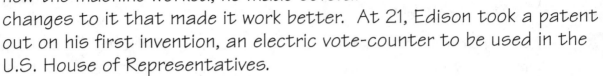

Thomas Edison was born to invent things. He had a curiosity about everything he touched. By the time he was 16, he had already taken apart a telegraph machine. Once he discovered how the machine worked, he made several changes to it that made it work better. At 21, Edison took a patent out on his first invention, an electric vote-counter to be used in the U.S. House of Representatives.

Many of Edison's inventions were among the most useful and helpful inventions ever created. He is responsible for inventing the electric light, the phonograph, the stock ticker, and the alkaline storage battery. We are able to enjoy motion pictures in theaters today because Edison invented the motion-picture projector. Many of his lesser inventions came easily. Others, such as the electric light bulb, required years of work by Edison and thousands of dollars to perfect.

Thomas Edison will always be remembered as the most productive inventor of all time. In 1882 alone, he applied for 141 patents, 75 of which were granted. Many inventors consider their careers successful if they invent even a few useful devices. When Edison died in 1931 at the age of 84, he had patented 1,093 inventions.

Fact vs. Opinion

Directions: "Pure Genius" contains both statements of fact and statements of opinion. Review the definitions below. Find two statements of fact and tell how you know they are facts. Find two statements of opinion and tell how you know they are opinions.

Fact ——→ something that exists, something that has actually occurred, or something known by observation or experience to be true or real

Opinion ——→ a conclusion or judgment that expresses how someone feels or thinks

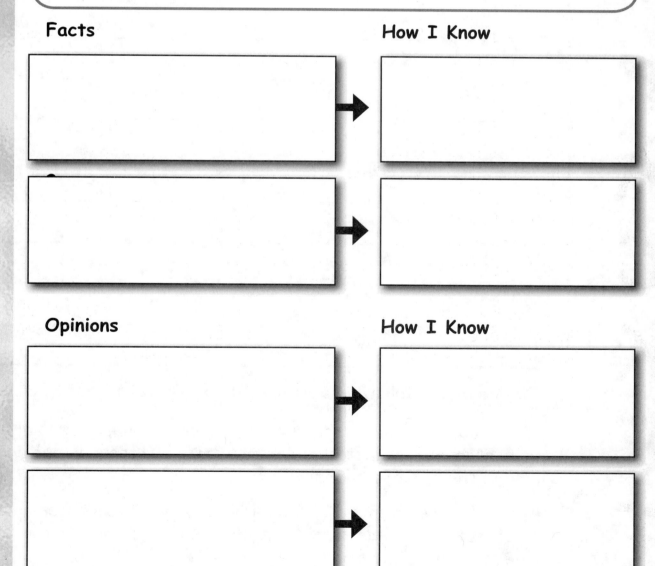

Facts

How I Know

Opinions

How I Know

The Back Page

Talk About It

Parent ➜ Ask your son or daughter the following question:

- How can you tell a statement of fact from a statement of opinion?

Student ➜ Answer the above question in complete sentences in the space below.

_____

_____

_____

_____

_____

_____

_____

➤ **Do one of the following activities on a separate piece of paper:**

- Cut out sentences from a magazine or newspaper that are statements of fact and opinion. Paste the facts in one column and the opinions in another.

- Write one statement of fact and tell why it is a statement of fact. Write one statement of opinion and tell why it is a statement of opinion.

P A L   P A C K E T

Answer Key

Page 10 — Finding the Similar and Opposite Ones
Responses will vary; accept all reasonable responses.

Underlined Word	Meaning	Synonym
blazing	brightly shining	glowing
respectful	feeling or showing care or concern	polite
cautiously	careful not to get in danger or make mistake	carefully
stunning	very attractive	beautiful

Underlined Word	Meaning	Antonym
immense	very large	tiny
valuable	worth something	worthless
firmly	not being able to move easily	loosely
rudely	without respect for others	politely

Underlined Word	Meaning	Homonym
peek	to take a quick look	peak
reins	a narrow strap of leather used to control a horse	rains
weather	the conditions outside	whether
knot	made by tying two pieces of something together, like string or rope	not

Page 36 — Putting the Events in the Right Order
First: A Native American woman was collecting corn.

Second: As the woman was leaving, she heard the voice of a child.

Third: The woman returned to look for the child, but found nothing.

Fourth: The woman left the cornfield but heard the voice again.

Fifth: The woman looked harder and found a forgotten ear of corn.

Sixth: The woman picked the tiny ear of corn, and since that day, no corn has been forgotten or wasted.

Page 38 — Story Sequencing
First: A large moose was drinking all the water in the river.

Second: The animals were worried, so they had a meeting to decide how to get rid of the moose.

Third: The animals didn't come up with a plan, but they were all too afraid to try anyway.

Fourth: The fly announced that he had a plan to make the moose leave.

Fifth: The other animals laughed and called the fly crazy.

Sixth: When the moose went to the river, the fly bit the moose over and over.

Seventh: The moose stamped the ground, and water filled up the holes.

Eighth: The moose couldn't stand the fly's biting, ran away, and never returned.

Ninth: The fly was proud and told the other animals that even small creatures can make a difference.

Page 54 — Fact or Opinion?
Opinion — The San Antonio Spurs are the best basketball team in the NBA.

Fact — Thomas Jefferson was the third president of the United States.

Opinion — That sunset was the most beautiful I have ever seen in my life.

Fact — Christopher Columbus is often considered the explorer who first discovered the Americas.

Fact — The Declaration of Independence was signed on July 4, 1776.

Opinion — The best and most popular president ever to lead our country was Abraham Lincoln.

Opinion — The best way to understand what you have read is to retell the story to someone.

Page 55 — Is That a Fact . . . or an Opinion?
Fact — The word *nimble* means "moving quickly and easily."

Fact — The blue whale is the largest mammal to ever live on earth.

Opinion — Peacock feathers are the prettiest kinds of feathers.

Fact — Oklahoma was the 46th state admitted into the United States.

Opinion — This summer won't be any fun if we don't have a pool to swim in.

Opinion — Barry Bonds is the greatest living baseball player.

Answer Key *(cont.)*

Page 55 *(cont.)*

Fact — In our solar system, the planet nearest to the sun is Mercury.

Page 70 —Name the Figurative Language

1. metaphor
2. personification
3. simile
4. imagery
5. simile
6. metaphor
7. simile
8. simile
9. imagery
10. metaphor
11. personification
12. metaphor
13. imagery
14. personification

Page 100 — Outline for "A Tunnel Built"

The Holland Tunnel

I. The Hudson River
  A. Commission set up in 1906
    1. Decided to build tunnel under Hudson
      a. Would be less affected by weather

II. Hudson River Vehicular Tunnel Project
  A. Clifford Holland
    1. Chosen in 1919 to lead project
    2. Construction began in 1920
  B. A challenge
    1. Fumes from cars harmful
    2. Automatic ventilation system
      a. Made air in tunnel clean
      b. Air cleaner than above ground
  C. First of its kind
    1. First fixed vehicle crossing from NYC to NJ
    2. First mechanically ventilated vehicle tunnel

III. 1924
  A. Clifford Holland dies
    1. Died one day before tunnels to meet

IV. Tunnel opens in 1927
  A. Called Holland Tunnel
    1. Named after Clifford Holland

  B. Toll 50 cents
  C. 1½ miles long
    1. Takes 8 minutes to pass through
  D. First day
    1. 51,694 vehicles passed through
  E. Cost
    1. $50 million
    2. Now would be $1.4 billion
  F. 1.3 billion vehicles have passed through so far

Page 102 — Timeline for "A Tunnel Built"

1906

Commission decides to build tunnel underneath the Hudson River from NYC to NJ

1919

Clifford Holland chosen to lead the "Hudson River Vehicular Tunnel Project"

1920

Construction begins on the tunnel; start building automatic ventilation system

1924

Clifford Holland dies; two tunnels from NYC and NJ linked together

1927

Holland Tunnel opens; toll is 50 cents; 51,694 vehicles pass through on the first day

Page 116 — Make Them Agree

1. wear
2. sleeps
3. talk
4. fits
5. enjoy
6. likes
7. is
8. were
9. cleans
10. buys

Page 117 — More Agreement Practice

1. walk, rule 4
2. jumps, rule 3
3. are, rule 5
4. try, rule 2
5. pretends, rule 1
6. eats, rule 1
7. hike, rule 4
8. go, rule 2

Answer Key *(cont.)*

Page 121 — Using Adjectives

These are suggested answers. Other combinations are possible and should be accepted.

1. Kent bought a <u>dozen</u> roses to give to his mom for her birthday.
2. Because of the rain, they had the <u>most dreadful</u> time at the party.
3. Hershel had the <u>craziest</u> idea about jumping off the bridge into Snake River.
4. Macy was <u>more nervous</u> than Anita about the dance recital.
5. The star of the show was even <u>more handsome</u> than I had imagined.
6. This was the <u>most cheerful</u> I had seen my father in days.
7. It seemed as if the mountains were a <u>million</u> miles away.
8. After the race ended, Tyrone had the <u>gloomiest</u> look on his face.
9. The <u>golden</u> sunlight shone upon the water like <u>gleaming</u> diamonds.
10. We had an <u>uneasy</u> feeling about going into the <u>mysterious</u> cave.

Page 122 — Using Adverbs

These are suggested answers. Other combinations are possible and should be accepted.

1. Frederick's parents left the key <u>underneath</u> the front-door mat.
2. My best friend, Felix, lives <u>nearby</u>, so we should go to see him.
3. <u>Immediately</u> after the game, we went to the ice cream shop.
4. The monkey <u>curiously</u> lifted the coconut off the ground.
5. She <u>awkwardly</u> grabbed hold of the mug before it fell.
6. Veronica <u>gradually</u> moved the bed to where she wanted it.
7. The school had most <u>recently</u> thrown a carnival to raise money for field trips.
8. He slept <u>more peacefully</u> today than yesterday since the wind had <u>finally</u> died down.

9. Meryl finally got a job at the bookstore after <u>regularly</u> shopping there over the past year.
10. I think she <u>especially</u> liked the chocolate-covered strawberries.

Page 126 — Let's Capitalize!

1. Mary and Joe spoke <u>Spanish</u> to each other during lunch.
2. One of the requirements for graduation is to take a <u>foreign language</u> class.
3. The children down the street know <u>Finnish</u> and <u>English</u>.
4. correct as is
5. correct as is
6. I hope to take a course in <u>Latin</u> when I start high school.
7. correct as is
8. correct as is
9. My father is <u>Mexican</u>.
10. The dancers were <u>Polynesian</u> and wore grass skirts.
11. Learning how to speak <u>Japanese</u> is difficult.
12. There are many different <u>nationalities</u> in the world.
13. The exchange student was <u>Belgian</u> and spoke <u>English</u> and <u>French</u>.
14. correct as is
15. There are many different <u>languages</u> that are <u>African</u>.

Page 127 — Your Turn to Capitalize

1. A good second language to learn is Spanish.
2. Her nationality is Peruvian.
3. We learned about some of the Romans in our history class.
4. If you want to learn Chinese, you will need to study harder.
5. Her native language is Farsi, not English.
6. She comes form Irish, German, and Swedish descent.
7. Some of her ancestors were British subjects.
8. I learned how to speak Italian while in college.

Answer Key (cont.)

Pages 132–134 — Punctuate It and Rewrite It!

1. On our trip, we went to New Mexico, Arizona, Nevada, and Utah.

2. Carly, these stories' endings were all the same.

3. "We arrived in plenty of time to see the show," whispered Cal.

4. Everyone's attention was focused on the airplane's wings.

5. Purple, blue, and red are my favorite colors.

6. We will be going home first, Dennis.

7. She picked up her book, threw it on the table, and stormed out.

8. Mr. and Mrs. Collins, here is the phone number you asked for.

9. "We will start building it," said Kelly, "but we will not finish it today."

10. The captain shouted, "All hands on deck!"

11. The salesmen's meeting was supposed to be tomorrow.

12. "I will be your best friend," replied Samara, "even after you move."

13. The waitress found the baby's bottle underneath the table.

14. Thank you, Dionne, for taking care of our cat, Snickers.

15. At the farm, Keith saw a horse, an ox, and a mule pulling a cart.

Page 141 — Verb Voyage

The notorious pirates were sailing on the ocean. The nervous captain saw them through his trusted telescope. "We are going to have to wage war!" said the captain loudly. The crew replied angrily, "We knew that the pirates would spoil our day!" The captain told his sailors to get the cannons ready for a battle. They had the cannonballs stacked and prepared to blast when the captain shouted, "Wait! These pirates are from Pittsburgh! Grab the bats!"

Page 142 — Superb Verbs

The girls were excited. Tonight they were going to see their favorite singing group, the Electric Hip Hops. "I just love the way T.K. sings 'You Are the Only Girl I Will Probably Forget,'" said Tracy. "Shamika likes it when Bobby sings 'I Was Crazy,'" said Maria. The parking lot was empty when they arrived at the stadium. Tracy looked at the tickets. "Oh no!" she said. "These tickets are for next week!"

Page 154 — Change Is Good!

1. sombreros
2. universities
3. salary
4. squash
5. igloos
6. six
7. chiefs
8. zero
9. trench
10. handkerchiefs
11. vanity
12. businesses
13. pulleys
14. knives
15. mattress

Page 155 — Change Is Good! (cont.)

1. She had promised to return his book.
2. Next Wednesday we are going to see them play baseball.
3. She bought her sweater last Thursday.
4. He saw the volcano erupt on a vacation with his parents.
5. The play we saw was wonderful.
6. me
7. Ours
8. my
9. our
10. mine